DEDICATION

To Lynne

Whose love is yet another natural wonder

Deadman's Island, above in 1898, was once thought to be part of
Stanley Park. It unfortunately wasn't. As a consequence, the
Island was stripped of its magnificent stands of fir and cedar.

CONTENTS

Stanley Park

Mike Steele

"A city that has been carved out of the forest should maintain somewhere within its boundaries evidence of what it once was, and so long as Stanley Park remains unspoiled that testimony to the giant trees which occupied the site of Vancouver in former days will remain."
Vancouver News-Herald, October 30, 1939

COVER PHOTO
Once the main means of transportation in Stanley Park, horse-drawn carriages are again a feature of Vancouver's most famous attraction.
Photo courtesy AAA Horse and Carriage, Ian Kim photographer.

COLOR SECTION
Ducks Unlimited Canada: 136 (top right), 137 (bottom); Kim, Ian: 134 (bottom), 135, 144 (top); Vancouver Public Aquarium: 133 (top left), 137 (top left), 138 (bottom), 139.
All others by author Mike Steele.

BLACK AND WHITE PHOTOS
B.C. Provincial Archives: 9, 10, 52; Cesar, Ed: 85 (top); City of Vancouver Archives: 3, 7, 14, 17, 29, 37 (top), 42 (top), 43, 48 (bottom), 53 (top), 78-79, 83, 90, 96-98, 105, 107 (top), 110-11, 121; Tourism B.C.: 20, 92; Vancouver Public Library: 5, 37 (bottom), 39, 42 (bottom), 48 (top), 52, 53 (bottom), 58, 68, 88-89, 102, 107 (bottom), 111 (bottom), 115, 116, 120; Wright, Richard: 85; Young, Peggy: 119, 123.

MAPS
Pages 130-131: Vancouver Board of Parks and Recreation.
All others courtesy Whitecap Books.

Copyright © 1993 Mike Steele

CANADIAN CATALOGUING IN PUBLICATION DATA

Steele, Richard M. (Richard Michael)
    Stanley Park

ISBN 1-895811-00-7

1. Stanley Park (B.C.) — History. 2. Stanley
Park (B.C.) — Guidebooks. I. Title.
FC3847.65.S84 1993   971.1' 33   C93-091111-3
F1089.5.V22S84 1993

First Edition - 1993

HERITAGE HOUSE PUBLISHING COMPANY LTD.
Box 1228, Station A, Surrey, B.C. V3S 2B3

Printed in Canada

The Georgia Street entrance in 1889.

INTRODUCTION

Since Stanley Park's official opening on September 27, 1888, it has gained an international reputation as one of the world's most spectacular and popular urban recreation areas.

A mecca for tourists and British Columbia residents alike, each year its zoos, aquarium and other facilities attract 2 to 3 million visitors, while some 7 to 8 million vehicles stream into the Park. As to the additional number of people who come simply to walk, swim, jog or cycle — well, there just isn't any way to determine a reasonable estimate, let alone an accurate figure.

The reasons for all this attention are numerous. Occupying the entire northwest end of the Burrard Peninsula, the Park provides a stunning variety of sea, mountain and city vistas, by day or night, in all seasons. Then there's the Park itself.

An amalgam of forest and meadow, wilderness and amusement area, Stanley Park's 405 ha (1,000 acres) are crisscrossed by trails and girdled by an 8.9-km (5.5-mile) Seawall promenade. It contains a small zoo as well as a children's petting zoo, an aquarium featuring the largest number of live specimens of any in North America, formal gardens, a miniature railroad, Native artifacts, restaurants, playgrounds, two beaches, two lakes, picnic spots, sports areas and massive trees that were already 600 years old — or more — when Canada became a nation in 1867.

Yet there is also another Stanley Park, one few people even suspect. For what is now a place of relaxation and amusement was once the home and burial ground of Coast Salish Natives, a projected battlefield for American and British forces, a haven of gold-seekers, a refuge for 19th century shipjumpers, the site of a forgotten (but still extant) pioneer cemetery, a cache for bank robbers and the reputed haunt of ghosts.

But while its present and much of its past are known, far less certain is this magnificent Park's future.

Several areas explored in this book are the subjects of an ongoing debate and may undergo substantial changes over the next few years. Among them are the main zoo — which could be upgraded, expanded or eliminated entirely — and Beaver Lake. Rapidly shrinking because of the introduction of non-native aquatic plants several decades ago, it will only survive as a water body for another decade or so unless dredged.

Then there is the problem of Stanley Park's popularity. It may force Vancouver park officials to shortly institute still other changes, one major and one relatively minor.

The first concerns possible restrictions on motor vehicle traffic: there are simply too many cars streaming through the park. On weekends and holidays, roadways are choked with frustrated motorists faced with a dearth of parking spots and bottlenecks at all exits. Private vehicles may be curtailed or, in some parts of the park at least, banned outright.

The second problem is the Seawall, Stanley Park's much-used perimeter path. Accidents involving cyclists and pedestrians, some resulting in serious injuries, led to the division of the Seawall several years ago. Separate lanes were established to prevent such occurrences. The experiment didn't work for a variety of reasons, including the increase in the numbers in both parties and a decidedly lackadaisical observance by each of the other's assigned track. Under consideration is a blanket prohibition against bicycles on the Seawall, a hotly contended solution.

But Stanley Park is no stranger to controversy and conflict.

Even in 1890 when the above photo was taken, the massive Western Red Cedar near the man was impressive. Now over 100 years older, it is one of the Park's most accessible forest giants. (See page 108.)

STANLEY PARK: A BRIEF NATURAL HISTORY

WATER, FIRE AND ICE

Stanley Park is, by any standard, an incredible achievement. But not all of the credit belongs to those who, for more than a century, have labored to create the park we know today.

The primary engineers of Stanley Park were water, fire and ice.

Stanley Park is the product of tremendous natural forces exerted over millions of years. At times in its geological history it has lain far below sea level, forced downwards by massive glacial ice sheets as much as 1,829 m (6,000 feet) thick. At other times, surging rivers of lava tore and burned their fiery way through the park peninsula.

This geological story of Stanley Park is a dramatic and violent one that begins some 140 million years ago. The coast of B.C was then little more than a series of marine basins and volcanic islands, the whole perched precariously over a foundation of molten material which periodically broke through weak spots in the fragile crust.

By 35-50 million years ago major changes had taken place. The local climate was wetter and warmer than now, resembling that of modern California. The plants which proliferated under such conditions left their own legacy deep in the Burrard Peninsula by eventually turning into the soft lignite seams which would, in the 20th century, lure entrepreneurs intent on transforming Stanley Park into a coal mine.

Also during this period the prominent sandstone bluffs of the Park's western rim were laid down as silt on the ocean floor.

Then the lava came, intruding through the sandstone to form veins, or "dykes," of dark grey stone and, where it met the colder water of English Bay, towering ranks of strangely symmetrical columns. The former created the pinnacle known as Siwash Rock; the latter, the sheer, colonnaded cliffs of Prospect Point.

Another change occurred with the cooling of the earth some 2 million years ago. Vast ice sheets began to stretch out across the world, at least three of these glacial advances extending down into this part of British Columbia.

The sands and gravels of Stanley Park date partly to this time, some pushed along in front of the glacial tongues, some borne by chilly rivers coursing under the glaciers. The bulk of these deposits arrived as recently as 20,000 to 50,000 years ago, accompanied by the blue-grey clay which lies just beneath the Park's surface and which would one day draw Coast Salish Natives who would fashion it into pipes smoked for ceremonial purposes.

While it may be difficult to imagine, so great were these frozen masses of ice that the land literally sank under their enormous weight, rising again with each glacier's retreat. Sections of the Lower Mainland, including the future Stanley Park, subsequently rebounded as much as 152 m (500 feet).

Only 11,000 years ago did the Burrard Peninsula shrug off its last icy mantle to allow the growth of the primeval forest whose modern descendant covers much of the Park's promontory.

Captain George Vancouver, above, in 1792 recorded Stanley Park as an island at the mouth of "Burrard's Canal," top right. He also placed Deadman's Island to the west of the Park rather than to the east.

THE HUMAN HISTORY OF STANLEY PARK

FOOTPRINTS IN THE FOREST

Much of what we claim to know about Stanley Park's pre-European history is little more than conjecture; no systematic, archaeological examination of the Park's identified Native sites has so far been undertaken. However, it is known that the Fraser River Delta, only a few miles away, was the scene of intense Native activity at least 9,000 years ago. Evidence suggests that similar extensive use of Stanley Park by indigenous peoples is within the realm of possibility.

In 1888, at Lumberman's Arch, an extremely large midden (in effect a garbage heap, but one with historical significance) composed mainly of broken shells, was quarried for surfacing material for the Park's first road. The remains of an old Native village still stood beside and on this midden.

Well over 2 m (8 feet) in depth and covering some 1.6 ha (4 acres), this midden's size alone indicated lengthy occupation of the beach-front location to the workmen involved in the project. But they were astounded to discover deep within the pile stumps of cedar trees 300 to 500 years old with roots firmly imbedded in still deeper Native shell deposits.

While we now believe that the village was a fairly recent addition, perhaps dating only to the 19th century, certainly Lumber-

9

man's Arch was an important site long before Natives chose to erect dwellings of a more permanent nature.

The Spaniards

The honor of discovering Stanley Park, insofar as the Europeans were concerned, went to the Spanish near the end of the 18th century.

Jose Maria Narvaez conducted a relatively cursory exploration of the inlet and its jutting peninsula in 1791. In 1792, Dionisio Alcala Galiano modified the charts of his predecessor and appears to

Coast Natives probably lived in the Stanley Park area as long as 9,000 years ago. Above are a warrior and a child, and, below, a village. The rope around the warrior's neck, their houses, and their canoes all came from the cedar tree.

have exchanged information with an English explorer he encountered, Captain George Vancouver.

Captain George Vancouver

Curiously, Captain Vancouver's maps of Stanley Park show it as an island sitting in the mouth of what he called "Burrard's Canal," now Burrard Inlet.

(He may have been right, despite the generally accepted belief that his depiction was a simple cartographical error. The narrow waist which today comprises Lost Lagoon and Ceperley Meadow-Second Beach was, until well into the 20th century, low-lying with a small stream running from English Bay to a tidal bay cutting deeply into the park from Coal Harbour on its southeast shore.)

Making his way in Burrard's Canal, Vancouver was greeted by Natives in dugout canoes who sprinkled white waterfowl down on the water. This action is seen by some modern interpreters as a form of welcome, by others as an attempt to ward off disaster.

Vancouver reported that he and his crew were unable to discern any signs of buildings, reinforcing the theory that Burrard Inlet at this point may have been solely a focus of traditional hunting-gathering.

Hudson's Bay Company and Gold

The area appears to have been ignored until 1851 when it was visited by John Muir, a Hudson's Bay Company employee dispatched to determine whether or not rumored coal deposits were of sufficient size and quality to warrant HBC interest. They weren't.

The next known reference to the park region does not occur until 1858. Then miners en route to the Fraser River gold rush in the Interior established a temporary camp at Second Beach which existed at least during the spring and summer of that year.

The American Threat

A decision that was to have a significant impact on the existence of a park was taken in 1859 when it was designated a Government Reserve.

War between Britain and the United States seemed imminent. It was believed that an American attack, if it came, would be a naval invasion launched through Burrard Inlet. American forces would sail down the broad waterway until they reached a point from which to launch an overland assault on New Westminster, then the capital of the Crown Colony of British Columbia.

The key to the success or failure of such a military operation was Stanley Park. By declaring the tip of the peninsula a Government Reserve, the British were guaranteed control of the heights at the mouth of the Inlet and a ready supply of trees with which to construct breastworks and other fortifications for artillery batteries.

Although the much-feared attack never came, the area's status as a Government Reserve sharply curtailed pioneer settlement. It was subsequently limited largely to the easternmost edges at what is now Brockton Point.

Loggers, Pioneers and Graves

The Reserve's thick forest, however, was not safeguarded. At least five small logging companies were active in Stanley Park from the 1860s through the 1880s. In fact, many of the Park's existing trails date to this period.

Logs were dragged out of the dense stands of fir, hemlock and cedar on muddy roads covered with rough planks (sometimes lubricated with dogfish oil) which were known as "skidroads." Ironically, virtually every major path that furnishes visitors an opportunity to stroll, cycle or jog through Stanley Park's awe-inspiring tall timber was originally nothing more than an avenue for logging operations.

Still, many of the large trees survived — although just barely.

In 1865, Captain Edward Stamp was thwarted in his attempts to operate a sawmill at Brockton Point, which would have made logging the entire park feasible, by treacherous currents along the Park's northern and northeastern flanks. Although he succeeded in clearing 40.5 ha (100 acres) there, he abandoned his plans when he discovered that it was impossible to maintain log booms (rafts of logs) in the swift waters of Burrard Narrows.

But the extensive opening he had made in the forest covering Brockton Point appealed to others. A small pioneer settlement appeared on the site in the early 1870s (more about that later), and in 1875 a Provincial Government employee named John Jane suggested that Stamp's "field of dreams" become the region's first cemetery. He gave the following explanation:

"...I think the inhabitants would be quite pleased to have this place chosen for a Grave Yard. Moreover it would answer for the entire Inlet. The land on the Granville Reserve [the townsite declared in 1870 whose name would be changed to Vancouver in 1886] is rather low and damp & I question if I shall be able to select a very favorable spot on it."

Canadian Pacific Railway Land Grab

A far greater threat to the park surfaced in 1885. The rapacious Canadian Pacific Railway, ever keen to increase its land holdings, sought to secure as much of the park as it could from the Canadian Government.

A letter, written in January by CPR Vice-President W.C. Van Horne to surveyor L.A. Hamilton, included a map detailing the portion of the park that the railway initially sought. A line was drawn across the then-Government Reserve from what is today the swimming pool at Second Beach all the way to the mouth of Beaver Lake Creek which exits on the northern side of the park between Prospect Point and Lumberman's Arch. Everything south and east of this line would be ceded to the CPR.

But as Van Horne revealed in his instructions to Hamilton, this letter appears to have been only the opening gambit in the CPR strategy:

"We are asking the Dominion Government for the strip of land on the peninsula at Coal Harbour.... The Minister of Militia requires a plan and description of this land, and I do not know whether or not the plan enclosed is sufficiently correct. Please send one that will do to go with an official communication. I would also like ... a general description of the peninsula, something that will enable the Department of Militia to determine how much of the ground should be retained by the Government for defensive purposes and how much they can spare us."

But the CPR, abruptly and seemingly inexplicably, dropped the project. That they did so was curious, especially in light of the CPR's notorious land-grabbing efforts throughout the building of the transcontinental railway. Yet there are tantalizing clues which may or may not account for this sudden disinterest, clues which might even explain why Stanley Park was created in the first place.

Who Needs A Park?

Some 16 months after Van Horne's letter to L.A. Hamilton, the newly minted City Council of the City of Vancouver passed its first resolution at 7:30 p.m. on May 12, 1886, stating:

"...that the Mayor be authorized to forward a petition to the Dominion Government through the Member for New Westminster District praying that the whole of that part of the Coal Harbour Peninsula known as the Government Reserve be conveyed to the City of Vancouver for a Public Park."

Interestingly, the motion was moved by the CPR's L.A. Hamilton. It was an odd choice as the first item of business, especially considering the context of Vancouver in 1886. Much of the urban area was heavily forested, the population centered on a limited waterfront quarter now known as Gastown.

The city itself had been incorporated only in April and, in June could claim just 2,600 inhabitants. There was certainly no pressing need for treed expanses or natural vistas when almost unbroken ranks of evergreens stretched north, south and east. Vancouver was merely a small clearing in an immense wilderness.

What they needed were docks and roads, health facilities and schools. Yet the primary goal of this governing body was the creation of a park. Or was it? Cynics believe that their real motive wasn't a park but protection of their own interests, beginning in 1862.

William Hailstone, Sam Brighouse and John Morton, the "Three Greenhorns" who staked the land abutting Stanley Park.

Below: The community of Granville — today's Vancouver — in 1886. The first order of business for the new "city" was to recommend establishing Stanley Park, a strange request for a community of 2,600 surrounded by wilderness. Was there an ulterior motive in the request? See page 13.

That year three pioneers — John Morton, William Hailstone and Samuel Brighouse — had established land claims that encompassed all of the current West End of Vancouver and the waterfront along Coal Harbour. They were jointly referred to as the "Three Greenhorns" because only greenhorns (an unflattering nickname applied to those lacking frontier knowledge) would be foolish enough to stake areas so far removed from what was then a tiny village to the east.

By 1886 their land was open (but covered in stumps and slash) and had been subdivided into rough lots, the whole called by the ambitious developers "New Liverpool." Few pieces had been sold and prospects seemed dim since the CPR had announced that its Pacific terminus would be Port Moody, not Vancouver.

The Three Greenhorns approached David Oppenheimer (who would serve three terms as Mayor of Vancouver) and asked him and a group of his business associates to lobby the CPR for an extension of the railhead to Vancouver. In return, Oppenheimer and his associates were given a part of the Greenhorns's holdings.

It is unclear whether Oppenheimer's group knew that the CPR had in fact already decided to carry the railway to Vancouver. They may have lobbied the company in good faith. Regardless, the CPR ended up with a percentage of the land held by the Oppenheimer cadre and the Three Greenhorns.

All three groups now had a vested interest in the parcels of property which abutted the Government Reserve, and all three had reason to fear the addition of the Reserve to an already saturated land market. The military had finally conceded that an American invasion was no longer likely and that the Reserve was unnecessary. Disposal possibilities included sale of the entire holding to development interests.

With the arrival of the railway, land prices would boom, especially if demand exceeded supply. The Reserve had to be kept off the market and the City Council's bizarre request for it to be preserved as parkland would ensure that it was.

Admittedly, the case is almost entirely circumstantial and some might describe it as mere fantasy. Yet there remains the tantalizing possibility that arguably the most beautiful urban park on the continent was created not out of altruistic or asthetic considerations but of simple, old-fashioned greed.

Approval and Expansion

By a Federal Order-In-Council on June 8, 1887, Vancouver's goal was realized: the Government Reserve could be used as parkland. Surprisingly, the eager L.A. Hamilton had already completed a survey for a road around it before this permission was even given.

The Park was officially opened on September 27, 1888. It was dedicated the following year on October 29 by the Governor-General of Canada, Lord Stanley, after whom the Park was named.

The City Council didn't entirely get its own way, though.

For the next 41 years a battle would be fought over whether or not Deadman's Island (now HMCS *Discovery)* was part of the grant. This small island in Coal Harbour is still alienated from the Park.

In 1908 the current 99-year lease went into effect in response to complaints from the Parks Board that the original agreement did not allow for long-term planning. (The Federal Government remains the Park's official landlord, receiving $1.00 a year for the lifetime of the renewable lease.)

In 1910 the park increased in size because of a decision by the City Council that: "...that land ... of the City lying on the South side of Coal Harbour and West of Chilco Street be placed under the control of the Parks Commissioners." The area referred to includes a daycare facility and the tennis courts located at the foot of Robson Street.

In 1913 a further addition was made when the Coal Basin, that part of Coal Harbour west of today's Causeway at the Georgia Street entrance was transferred first to the city, and then to the Parks Board. At the time little more than muddy tidal flats open to Coal Harbour, it became Lost Lagoon.

In the 1920s, the Squatter Eviction Trials in which the City, the Federal Government and the Parks Board sought the eviction of all residents of the Park resulted in the somewhat unusual addition of a small parcel of land (.4 ha, or 1 acre) at Lumberman's Arch.

This parcel was the only one within the former Government Reserve to which squatter's rights were found to apply. A woman known as Aunt Sally proved that she had occupied the property for 60 years which, according to law, gave her title to the site.

It was bought late in 1925 for $15,500 by W.C. Shelley, a Parks Board Commissioner, prominent Vancouver businessman and future provincial finance minister. Shelley took this unprecedented step to prevent the land being sold to developers who, it was believed, would construct an apartment building. Shelley subsequently turned it over to the Parks Board for inclusion in the Stanley Park holdings.

On December 30, 1929, the City's request that it be granted jurisdiction over Deadman's Island was realized. A Privy Council decision in Ottawa on January 23, 1930, read "...a ninety-nine year lease of Deadman's Island" had been issued "on condition that it be used exclusively for park purposes and given a proper name."

(Don't look for Deadman's Island on any official Board of Parks and Recreation map today. Citing wartime needs, on June 24, 1942, the Government "temporarily" transferred this picturesque is-

Building the Seawall around Siwash Rock in 1963. The man in the cap near center is James Cunningham, the master stonemason who for 32 years supervised construction. He is commemorated by a plaque at Siwash Rock.

land back to its own control. That September it terminated the lease and has controlled Deadman's Island ever since.)

The next land transfer occurred in 1939. The series of terraces at Prospect Point had been used for a signal station by the Federal Harbour Board until the erection of the Lions Gate Bridge eliminated any need for the structure. Control of the site passed to the Parks Board and Stanley Park grew yet again.

Because of an oversight, however, as recently as 1984 Stanley Park was still technically classified a "temporary park." But after questions were raised about the Vancouver Board of Parks and Recreation's jurisdiction, this status was belatedly upgraded to "permanent park."

There are also four areas of the park which are assumed to be part of it but which are not: the sites of Prospect Point and Brockton Point Lighthouses which fall under Federal authority, the footings at the south end of the Lions Gate Bridge, and the Bridge Highway which connects Georgia Street to the Lions Gate Bridge. The last two are administered by the provincial Department of Highways.

Access & Services

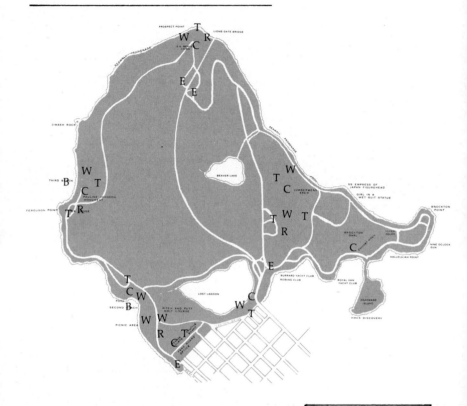

R	Restaurant
E	Entrance
T	Telephone
C	Concession Stand
W	Washroom
B	Beach

Destinations & Parking

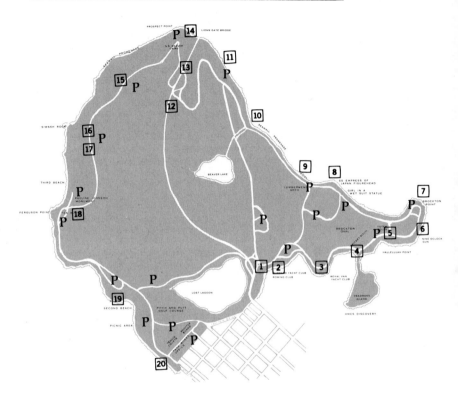

DESTINATION	DISTANCE		
	KM./MI.		
Starting Point: Promenade [1]	0/0	Exit to Lions Gate Bridge [12]	4.9/3.0
Zoo Turn-Off [2]	.16/.1	Bridge Highway Cross-over [13]	5.2/3.2
Royal Van. Yacht Club [3]	.7/.4	Prospect Point [14]	5.4/3.3
Deadman's Island [4]	1.1/.7	"Reservoir" Picnic Area [15]	6.0/3.7
Totem Poles [5]	1.3/.8	Hollow Tree [16]	6.3/3.9
Nine O'Clock Gun [6]	1.5/.95	"National Geographic" Tree [17]	6.5/4.0
Brockton Point [7]	1.8/1.1	Ferguson Point/Tea House/ [18]	7.3/4.5
Empress of Japan figurehead [8]	2.8/1.7	Third Beach	
Lumbermen's Arch [9]	3.0/1.85	Second Beach & Coal Harbour	
Beaver Lake Creek [10]	3.6/2.2	Road Turnoff [19]	8.4/5.2
"Chaythoos" [11]	4.1/2.5	Beach Avenue Entry/Exit [20]	9.1/5.6

P   Parking Lots; all no charge except at
Beach House Restaurant

19

The very popular Seawall offers scenery from Vancouver's skyline to unpenned wildlife, wilderness to 80,000-ton cruise ships sailing under Lions Gate Bridge.

STANLEY PARK WALKS: I

THE SEAWALL

The 8.9-km (5.5-mi.) Seawall pathway is the most popular trail with joggers, walkers and runners in Stanley Park. It is also completely wheelchair accessible.

This paved promenade tops a protective wall running around the Park with the exception of the narrow neck, or waist, at the Park's southern extreme. By day it provides sweeping, unobstructed views of Coal Harbour and Vancouver, Burrard Inlet, the North Shore and Coast Mountain Range, English Bay, and even Vancouver Island some 50 km (30 miles) away. At night (access is permitted to all park trails 24 hours a day) the panoramic displays of city lights and of ships at anchor in the harbour and English Bay are an unforgettable sight.

The Seawall Walk will take you past the sites of former pioneer and Native villages, lighthouses, picnic grounds, shipwreck locations, a children's water park, lava flows, a seabird colony, kelp beds favored by harbour seals, a salmon spawning stream and a wealth of other fascinating natural and crafted features.

If you have time for only one walk in Stanley Park, this is the one to take. It is the longest walk described, requiring an hour and a half to two hours to complete without stopping. To help locate prominent features along its length, in this book the Seawall Walk's major points of interest have been assigned numbers which correspond with those on the map on the next pages. The numbers are counter-clockwise from the Georgia Street entrance (1) to Beach Avenue on English Bay (50).

The Seawall: A Short History

Initially the Seawall was to have been only a 125-m (136-yard) stretch of granite designed to stop shore erosion caused by the wakes of passing ships and the constant hammering of waves.

But the year after this first small section was built in 1917, Park Superintendent W.S. Rawlings espoused something far more ambitious: a buffer and pathway along the entire Stanley Park foreshore:

"...it is not difficult to imagine what the realization of such an undertaking would mean to the attractions of the park," he wrote, "and personally I doubt that there exists anywhere on this Continent such possibilities of a combined park and marine walk as we have in the making in Stanley Park."

It would take 62 years for Rawlings' inspired dream to become reality.

The Seawall was built in sections as funding permitted. In 1920, the peak year for construction, over 2,300 men labored on it. Then during the Great Depression of the 1930s, gangs of relief workers toiled with sledges, chisels and drills to cut and set the 45.5-kg (100-pound) blocks in place. Since the work was performed whenever tides and Federal funding permitted, much of the seawall was extended during the winter months. Crews, who were at the mercy of the tides, often hammered and hoisted throughout the night.

For one 32-year period, Master Stonemason James Cunningham oversaw the building and became something of a local legend. His lengthy tenure created a bond that continued long past retirement. Although in poor health, the elderly gentleman would leave his bed clad only in topcoat and pajamas to direct the slow crawl of the Seawall along the Park's perimeter.

Like the wall's founder, Cunningham did not live to see his life's work finished. He died in 1963 and a plaque at Siwash Rock (35) commemorates his contribution. Sadly, history has been far less generous with Rawlings. He remains unrecognized.

The Walk Begins

We begin this marine stroll at Devonian Park (1), a small but attractive city park located on the border of Stanley Park at Georgia Street.

From here the visitor can gaze across the bay known as Coal

Walk I—The Seawall

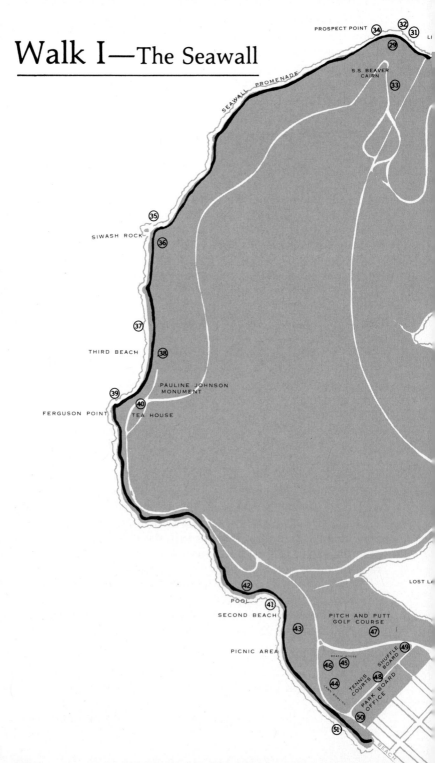

PROSPECT POINT

SEAWALL PROMENADE

S.S. BEAVER CAIRN

SIWASH ROCK

THIRD BEACH

PAULINE JOHNSON MONUMENT

FERGUSON POINT

TEA HOUSE

POOL

SECOND BEACH

PICNIC AREA

PITCH AND PUTT GOLF COURSE

LOST LA

BEACH HOUSE

TENNIS COURTS

SHUFFLE BOARD

PARK BOARD OFFICE

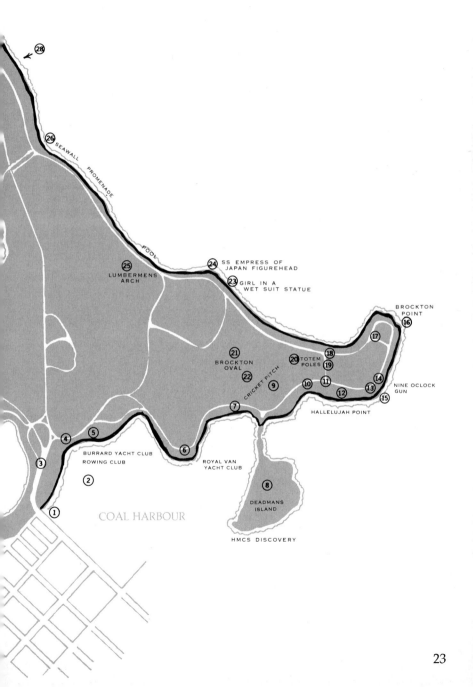

28

26 SEAWALL PROMENADE

POOL

25 LUMBERMENS ARCH

24 SS EMPRESS OF JAPAN FIGUREHEAD

23 GIRL IN A WET SUIT STATUE

BROCKTON POINT

16

17

21 BROCKTON OVAL

22

CRICKET PITCH

20 TOTEM POLES

18

19

9

10

11

14

13

12

15 NINE OCLOCK GUN

7

HALLELUJAH POINT

4

5

BURRARD YACHT CLUB
ROWING CLUB

6

ROYAL VAN YACHT CLUB

3

2

8

DEADMANS ISLAND

1

COAL HARBOUR

HMCS DISCOVERY

23

Harbour (2) which defines the southern shore of Stanley Park and which has featured prominently in its history.

Coal Harbour (2)

For roughly the next 2 km (1.2 miles), from the park entrance to roughly the Brockton Point Lighthouse, the Seawall skirts the northern edge of Coal Harbour.

This protected bay derives its name from deposits of low-grade coal found along its southern shore in 1859 by Captain George Richards of the British survey ship, HMS *Plumper*. Brockton Point bears the name of the *Plumper's* engineer, while Stanley Park and the adjacent area were subsequently — if briefly — referred to on naval charts as Coal Peninsula.

The Coal Harbour of Richards' time was far different from the one today. In place of expensive pleasure boats, the waters teemed with herring. Even in the 1860s and 1870s whales hunted in the bight and the clam-rich mud flats drew Natives from as far away as Howe Sound.

The bay also extended farther than it now does: the former head of Coal Harbour included Lost Lagoon (see Walk V). Until a bridge was authorized in 1888, visitors were forced to cross a large log at this point. Only many years later was the area where the visitor now stands filled to create the roadway (3) that leads from Vancouver to the Lions Gate Bridge and the park entryway.

The Vancouver Rowing Club (4)

Barely inside Stanley Park is a large building perched on piles, the Vancouver Rowing Club's quarters. Located here in 1905, the VRC is a park institution. Its forerunner, the Vancouver Boating Club, was founded in 1886 and merged with the Burrard Inlet Rowing Club under the current name in 1899.

The present clubhouse is not the original one. The first, a floating building which had the dubious distinction of having been commandeered by the city and towed to Deadman's Island in 1887 to house smallpox quarantine victims, was understandably replaced by a new one in 1888. The present one is a Heritage structure built in 1911. Members of the Vancouver Rowing Club have been earning gold, silver and bronze medals since the Paris Olympics in 1924.

Native Middens (5)

Stanley Park has a number of officially recognized former sites of temporary and/or permanent use by Aboriginal Peoples. Bordering this section of the walk, from approximately the Vancouver Rowing Club to the Royal Vancouver Yacht Club and the entrance to Deadman's Island-HMCS *Discovery* are several large middens which indicate such sites.

Middens are mounds of what anthropologists term "cultural material." While in some parts of the province middens were used for burials, the ones along most of the coast were nothing more than garbage heaps. Still, middens contain valuable clues to tools, foodstuffs and many other facets of Native life and are therefore protected by law.

From the Rowing Club to Deadman's Island you'll be walking past or on what is either a series of middens or one enormous one. Incidental discoveries in the past have yielded broken shells, fire ash, animal bones and stone tool flakes. Burrowing animals such as moles often push such material to the surface where it is readily recognizable to skilled eyes.

Royal Vancouver Yacht Club (6)

This small headland was occupied by a succession of pioneers over the years long before the RVYC appeared in 1905.

It was farmed by a settler named Anderson, probably into the early 1880s, but Anderson wasn't well known in the area and apparently left no records of his homestead. Following his death, "Anderson's Point" was taken over by Chinese pioneers who ran what was termed a "pig ranch" until late in 1890. Little is known of them either, in large part because the Chinese were the victims of widespread and systematic racism.

In 1888, for instance, with smallpox running through the homes in the new Park, the Health Inspector for Vancouver compiled a list of all dwellings to be destroyed in an effort to contain the disease. He listed the habitations, ascribing to each a compensation value — except for those at Anderson's Point. There he listed only "...a number of Chinese dens ... of no particular value."

In 1890 the Parks Board resolved: "That the Health Inspector be requested to take the necessary steps to have the Chinese expelled from the Park." With visits from the Chief of Police, the Health Inspector was able to report in August the same year that the Chinese had "agreed" to leave their ranch.

Two years later the Board was informed that "...the Park Ranger complains that the Chinese are in the habit of lighting fires in the vicinity of Chinese graves in the Park thereby endangering park property."

On instructions from the Parks Board, the Chief of Police ordered the Chinese to dig up their graves, located here and at Brockton Point (16), and to remove the bodies. Graves of Europeans were not disturbed.

The only other item of note at this site is that following the Chinese expulsion in 1890, the former pig ranch was converted into a buffalo paddock. Now it is the location of the RVYC parking lot.

Midden's End (7)

The end of the single midden, or perhaps series of middens, already mentioned occurs here, just before a very large, whitish boulder situated near the edge of the Seawall on the water side.

Deadman's Island (8)

As already noted, there is no indication that this islet, so tantalizingly close to the Stanley Park shore, bears the sinister-sounding name "Deadman's Island."

The entrance to what is now a restricted-access military base is marked by a guard hut, an ornamental fence and a sign declaring this to be HMCS *Discovery*. The title is rather ironic since visitors intent on discovering anything beyond this point risk prosecution.

The Island of Dead Men

Sailors and others have left quite extensive descriptions of the Island, dating back to the late 18th century. What they described was a place populated exclusively by the dead.

Cedar bentwood boxes containing the remains of Native chiefs and others were in the branches of many of the towering trees which once covered the Island. Deep in the shade and gloom of the undergrowth were many more boxes and similar structures, all serving as tombs.

John Morton, one of the Three Greenhorns who established Vancouver's West End, rowed over to the Island in 1865 to examine these containers to learn what they held. Reaching up with a fallen tree limb, he poked one of the funeral chests sitting on an overhead branch. To his horror the rotting box disintegrated, showering him with human bones and other debris. He fled back to his boat and quickly rowed home.

The lonely islet obviously left an impression on Morton. He not only attempted to buy it but also to learn the reason for its unusual name. He consequently met with a Squamish chief who told him it was not for sale but offered the following story:

According to the Chief, a battle had been fought long ago between local Natives and those "from the north." Women and children from the Burrard Inlet faction were captured and held on the Island. The northerners agreed to free their captives in return for the surrender of the opposing warriors. Once the exchange was consummated, the hapless warriors — reputedly 200 in number — were slaughtered. The site was thereafter known as the Island of Dead Men.

(The Reverend Charles Tate, one of the earliest missionaries and fluent in Native dialects, recorded the Island's name as "Memloose-Siwash-il-la-hie" which he believed to mean either "Indian Graveyard" or "Village of Dead Men.")

Following the visit of HMS *Plumper* in 1859 it was shown on some maps as Coal Island. But Dead Man's Island and, more often, Deadman's Island predominated. In the years immediately after Morton's dramatic visit, the Island saw little change. Fishermen dried their nets there and Peter the Whaler, a Portuguese squatter from Brockton Point (16), occasionally rendered blubber on the beach from whales he and his mixed Native and Hawaiian crew killed in what would become Vancouver Harbour. Natives and non-Natives continued to use Deadman's Island as a cemetery.

The Plague Years
In January 1888 smallpox was detected throughout the Vancouver area and by April quarantines were in effect. The City of Vancouver, badly in need of an isolated site to separate the diseased from the rest of the populace, chose Deadman's Island.

During the next two years, a number of smallpox victims were buried on the Island, despite the 1887 opening of an official cemetery at Mountainview in Vancouver. Unless the graves were disturbed by subsequent military construction, the bodies must still be there since they were never exhumed by civic authorities or next-of-kin.

A young English remittance man, confined on the Island during this period, wrote to his mother, giving as his address "The Pest House, Deadman's Island, Vancouver, British Columbia." It's not too difficult to imagine how she must have taken this macabre indication of how her son was faring in the New World.

Howls, Hookers and Hubris
As far as city officials were concerned they had found an easy solution to a serious health problem, but the semi-autonomous Parks Committee was outraged. It considered the Island part of Stanley Park. (The Vancouver Board of Parks and Recreation was previously known by a succession of titles. For simplicity, "Parks Board" will be used for the remainder of this book, even though this title may not have been the correct one in a given period.)

Things grew even more heated when it was discovered that sick prostitutes from Vancouver's red light district were being housed on Deadman's Island. A power struggle developed as the rival entities — the City of Vancouver and the Parks Board — vied to gain the upper hand in a political tug-of-war. Adding to its woes, the pugilistic Parks Board was engaged on another front.

Board members contended that their lease to Stanley Park included Deadman's Island. The Federal Department of Defence and Militia disagreed. It claimed the Island was still under its control as a Government Reserve and that an artillery battery would soon be built there. Shortly after, the military announced that it had changed its mind. A gunpowder magazine would be constructed instead.

Citizens and politicians combined forces in noisy protest. The Department of Defence immediately rescinded the decision, defusing at least one potentially explosive situation.

Prelude To Battle

Unfortunately, this decision wasn't the end of disputes over Deadman's Island. In fact, it was only the beginning of the most bizarre episode in Stanley Park's history — the sometimes deadly and often comical series of events the press would dub "The Battle of Deadman's Island." This "Battle" would be featured, and lampooned, in newspapers around the world.

With the end of the smallpox epidemic and apparent city interest, in January 1890 Park authorities set about building a bridge to the Island. What they didn't know was that since the previous January, an American industrialist from Seattle named Theodore Ludgate had been pressing the Department of Defence for a lease to the same property. He wanted to build a sawmill there within easy reach of port facilities across the harbor.

While the military waffled, Park crews cleared trails and laid out a picnic area. Then, in 1899, disaster struck. Ludgate's lease had been granted.

Parks officials denounced the encroachment on "their" lease. City authorities protested the move because they still regarded the Island as city land and intended building a drydock there.

Private citizens were sharply divided into pro- and anti-Ludgate sides. Within two weeks of the announcement, the issue was being debated at mass meetings. Even the local newspapers joined the fray. The *Vancouver Daily News-Advertiser* called one such gathering "...a sham rigged by the supporters and minions of the industrialist."

Then the Provincial Government intervened, challenging the Federal Government's right to assign any lease to land the legislature declared was under provincial jurisdiction.

Ludgate ignored them all. He was being charged $500 a year for his lease and had waited 10 years to get it. Now was the time for action. On April 24, 1899, he landed on Deadman's Island with a logging crew and began clear-cutting the ancient trees.

An irate Mayor Garden stormed over with a contingent of police and ordered Ludgate and his men to desist. Ludgate refused, personally wielding an axe to show his defiance. He was promptly arrested.

Although the charges were subsequently dropped by a magistrate uncertain who did control the Island, Ludgate was enraged. On May 15 he returned to Deadman's Island with a larger crew of loggers and again began falling and clearing. He informed the soli-

Theodore Ludgate, whose attempts to develop Deadman's Island started years of fighting and legal skirmishing that became known as the "Battle of Deadman's Island." The last tree on the disputed acreage was gone by 1911 and the last squatter evicted the next year. A second village evolved, below, and spread along the entire western shore but also was eventually moved.

tary guard left behind to forestall such action that he would stay "...until removed by force."

He got his wish.

City police arrived and arrested the loggers. Repeating that he would go only if forced — and manacled — Ludgate suffered both and was carried off to jail. Again.

But the "Ludgate Affair," as it was more soberly called, was not over. In 1906 the Federal Privy Council affirmed Ottawa's right to grant the lease. In 1908, Ludgate's agreement was amended to allow him to use the Island for purposes other than milling if he wished.

Perhaps tired of the wrangling, he offered to sell his lease to the City of Vancouver for $300,000. Considering that he hadn't even paid Ottawa any of the rents he owed, it was an audacious move worthy of grudging admiration.

The proposal was accompanied by a veiled threat that "...an amusement company of New York has made an offer for the ground with the intention of establishing thereon a large resort, something on the plan of Luna Park in Seattle." The city refused to rise to the bait.

In April 1909, Ludgate and E.L. Kinman, a Vancouver businessman, formed a syndicate and announced plans to begin work on a new, unspecified project on the Island. Parks Board placed guards on the property.

Ludgate tried unsuccessfully to have them removed and Kinman revealed that it was the syndicate's intention to build a $300,000 resort on the Island, complete with hotel and promenades. To this end, he secured eviction notices to oust the estimated 150 squatters who had taken up residence along its foreshore and beach.

The Battle of Deadman's Island

In late May, Kinman ordered the Park guards off. They refused to go. Then Park Superintendent G. Eldon and two employees acting as guards were thrown off the Island by Kinman and 10 of his hired men. Next day Kinman and a logging crew arrived to begin work, only to find access denied by a lone Constable.

Faced by a large group of what newspaper reporters would smirkingly refer to as "Kinman's Constable Chasers," the policeman drew his firearm and ordered them to advance no further. Kinman scoffed at the threat, informing the peace officer that "You cannot bluff me. I have looked down the business end of a gun before."

The Constable evidently believed him. He retreated hastily to an abandoned squatter's shack and barred the door. Within minutes what the press gleefully recorded as the "Commander" of the "First Ludgate Army," (and alternately "Battleaxe Brigade") had his men smash down the door, eject the Constable and throw him off the Island.

An enterprising reporter rowed over to interview Kinman, asking him what he intended to do should the police force arrive for revenge. Kinman, fists on hips and legs firmly astride, replied, "We will repel all boarders."

He was apparently looking for a fight. On May 31 he announced that only six squatters' shacks and half of Deadman's Island's trees remained. Shortly before 10:00 a.m. the following morning, the City took up the gauntlet.

Kinman was on the eastern shore of the Island when Police Chief Chamberlain, at the time also acting Mayor of Vancouver, several assistants and 12 uniformed police arrived on the tugboat *Hydra*. Chamberlain said that he had a warrant for Kinman's arrest on the charge of having assaulted a police officer.

Kinman, with only six men, agreed to go peacefully but grumbled that it took "...fifteen policemen and a bum politician" to remove him.

The next scene in what the press now generally called "The Battle of Deadman's Island" opened that afternoon.

Free on bail, Kinman landed on the opposite shore to that patrolled by police constables Allen, Lowry and Kuner. Armed with cudgels, the syndicate boss and his two companions surprised the officers. They were overwhelmed and beaten. Police reinforcements soon ensured that the three attackers spent an uncomfortable night in the Vancouver jail, a night which proved unnerving for the beefed-up police patrols assigned to prevent the Island from falling into "enemy" hands.

The policemen claimed that after sunset they heard "...bones of dead men rattling ... and skeletons stalked about in the dark, emitting blood-curdling shrieks and threatening to haunt those who were desecrating their graves by cutting down the trees that were protecting their rest from the storms of the Inlet."

The Chief of Police acidly retorted that perhaps his men would be braver if they had torches and the "phantoms" less bold because of them.

Kinman's lawyer brought suit against the city for what was claimed to be wrongful ejection of the syndicate from its property, adding that insult had been added to injury when their cook and field kitchen had been commandeered. The police smugly replied that both were "...spoils of war."

(A sheriff who approached the Island on June 10 was met by 18 nervous policemen at the landing stage. The amused law officer informed them that he was only there to ensure that the remaining squatters were evicted.)

Ludgate finally won his latest court case in 1910 but the issue still wasn't settled. In 1911, Ottawa asked former Vancouver City Solicitor George Cowan to report on the legality of the original lease signed by the then-Minister of the Militia, Sir Frederick Borden. Cowan's opinion, accepted by the Department of Justice, was that the first lease had indeed been legal but that subsequent amendments and extensions had not.

But why the Federal Government would question its own lease at all was a puzzle only solved many years later. According to Cowan, the new Minister of the Militia, Sir Sam Hughes, he and Kinman were seated in Hughes's office discussing plans the syndicate had for Deadman's Island. As Cowan related:

"Sir Sam had lauded the beauties of Deadman's Island because of its magnificent old cedar and pine trees, and said that it would be a crime to destroy such a beauty spot. Kinman turned to the minister, remarking 'It is a beauty spot no longer for I think that just about this moment the last of the trees will be cut down.'

"Sir Sam jumped to his feet, his face flushed with anger and, clenching his fist at Kinman, retorted: 'If that is so, you have acted like a vandal and this is the last visit you will make to my office!'

"Whereupon he turned to Cowan and instructed him to proceed with an action to nullify the syndicate's lease."

Ludgate appealed all the way to the Privy Council in London, England. Although he was able to retain the right to build a sawmill on the Island, slumping lumber markets made this project unfeasible.

In 1924 his lease expired and with it the Ludgate Affair, undoubtedly to the relief of all but newspapermen.

Squatters, Spooks and Sailors

Squatters began moving back onto the denuded Island even before the final court salvoes, primarily setting up home on the site of the former unauthorized village on the western shore.

In January 1929, the Parks Board's request for a lease to Deadman's Island was approved. The land would be leased to the City of Vancouver for 99 years at $1.00 a year for "park purposes" on the condition that a "suitable name" be found for it. The Board was prepared to rename it "Park Island" if the Federal Government could not be persuaded to let the existing name remain. But Ottawa did back down and Deadman's Island became official.

The first action of the park authorities was to seek eviction of the squatters. The new village was quite substantial by this time, although it was without running water, electricity or a replacement for the bridge which had long ago succumbed to old age.

Still, it was a thriving community which included many families. The children were taken by boat to either the Stanley Park shore or the foot of Georgia Street, walking the rest of the way to school in Vancouver's West End. It was, according to some of these surviving commuters, a thoroughly enjoyable place for young ones to grow up.

Unfortunately, this all came to an end after the posting of eviction notices in December 1930.

While the Parks Board now had a free rein, it really couldn't decide what to do with the Island in its current state. The 1930's Depression Years were eroding the Park's budget so extensive landscaping was ruled out. But there were plenty of other propositions from the citizenry and would-be entrepreneurs.

In 1932, a museum was suggested for the site, then in 1933 a dancehall application was refused. In 1936, someone suggested the novel idea of planting trees. But one of the more ironic proposals was the offer in 1930 from Theodore Ludgate's widow. She wanted to build a drinking fountain and teahouse in memory of her husband, presumably blissfully unaware of how her former husband was regarded by local residents.

In 1939, Deadman's Island was considered a possible site for troop barracks; in 1941, the campus of a military college. But in June 1942, it was transferred by a Federal Order-in-Council to the Department of National Defence as a base for the Royal Canadian Naval Volunteer Reserve. Several months later, the navy announced that a permanent installation was planned and on June 26, 1943, the cornerstone of HMCS *Discovery* was laid.

The Island has been occupied by the military ever since — but not peacefully. In the late 1980s attempts were made by the Parks Board, concerned citizens and several Federal Members of Parliament to have Deadman's Island transferred to Vancouver as a Centennial "gift." Unfortunately, political enthusiasm for the project dissipated when the property became a Native Land Claims issue.

Today, Deadman's Island seems almost deserted. The white-painted drill-hall and barracks stand empty most of the year and little activity occurs on the sedentary naval outpost. An exception, however, is the hauntings.

Base scuttlebut is that a weird spectral glow which gradually takes on human form is sometimes seen in the trees of Deadman's Island. This apparition is supposedly the spirit of a despondent seaman who hanged himself there. He is routinely blamed whenever personal effects and office equipment are moved or missing.

One change over the years is that the Island is smaller than it once was. In 1863 the Royal Engineers gave its area as 3.2 ha (8 acres). Erosion has claimed some of this land, apparently reducing the total to 2.8 ha (7 acres).

In addition, as is the case with much of Stanley Park's history, nothing in the immediate area officially notes Deadman's Island's former association with the Park, or the controversy which surrounded it over several decades. Still, the past has a way of subtly making itself known.

Every spring the wild remnants of pioneers' gardens, nearly lost in a tangle of weeds and debris, bloom again along Deadman's Island's western shoreline in colorful, if poignant, memorial.

Brockton Point (9)

Technically, "Brockton Point" refers only to the easternmost tip of this peninsula but to local users it comprises the Brockton Oval sports area, the Nine O'Clock Gun, the Totem Poles, the Chehalis Monument, Hallelujah Point and the Brockton Point Lighthouse. Yet few of these regular visitors realize that this focus of so much tourist activity was once the site of a thriving community.

Fishermen's Cove (10)

Immediately upon leaving the entrance to HMCS *Discovery*-Deadman's Island, the Seawall curves fairly sharply inwards to embrace a broad bay. The manicured expanse of lawn from here to the far side of the Totem Poles was once variously known as the Indian village, Settler's Cove, the Indian Portage and Fishermen's Cove. It was one of the oldest settlements on Burrard Inlet.

John Morton, one of the Three Greenhorns already mentioned, provided one of the earliest accounts of a European presence. Morton arrived in the Inlet by ship from Vancouver Island with a party of miners bound for the Cariboo gold fields on June 25, 1862. As they sailed past Lumberman's Arch (25) on the then-Government Reserve's north shore, they noticed that the "Indians" were engaged in a potlatch (a Native celebration and feast) but that several of those enjoying the festivities were bearded white men. Morton would be incorrectly informed that they were runaway Spanish sailors.

The bearded men were indeed runaway sailors but they weren't Spanish. They were Portuguese shipjumpers and Brockton Point's non-Native pioneers. Years later, during the Squatter Eviction Trials of the 1920s (more about this episode shortly) a descendant of one of these men would testify that her father, Peter Smith, had arrived at Brockton Point in 1860. Best known as Peter the Whaler, he had probably landed with a fellow countryman named DeCosta. Both married Native women and built the first houses at Brockton Point's Fishermen's Cove.

The sandy beach was ideal for hauling up boats or nets bursting with herring scooped from Coal Harbour. In the course of the next few decades their homes would be joined by others, some erected by other Portuguese expatriots.

In 1865 the original homesteads were threatened briefly by a sawmill planned by Captain Edward Stamp, but the entrepreneur's ambitious enterprise went no further than clearing some of the dense forest which covered Brockton Point. This clearing led to an influx of settlers, including Joseph Mannion who, with his Native wife, constructed a house near the present location of the Totem Poles (20).

One of the better known of the new arrivals was Joe Silvia who came to Fishermen's Cove in 1870. He was called Portuguese Joe #1 by largely British contemporaries to distinguish him from subsequent "Portuguese Joes" on the Inlet.

Silvia took a Native wife, a woman from the Musqueam band named Khaal-tin-aht. Following her death some years later, he again married a Native woman (intermarriage was the norm for Brockton Point settlers), Lucy Kwatleemat of Sechelt.

Portuguese Joe #1 supported his family by catching herring and dogfish, the oil of which was used to grease cedar-planked logging roads. According to one of his daughters, he also taught other Native women at Fishermen's Cove how to make and mend fishing nets. Around 1875, he passed his house on to Joseph Gonsalves, Portuguese Joe #3, to join an uncle, Portuguese Joe #2, in running a store in frontier Gastown, or Granville, better known as today's Vancouver.

Thomkins Brew also moved to Brockton Point in 1874 with his wife on his retirement from active duty as the first police constable and customs officer on Burrard Inlet. The couple raised a few cows, selling milk to Gastown denizens who possibly thought it a novelty compared to their preferred staples of rotgut whiskey and gin.

About the same time, the growing village received an influx of new residents. They were four sailors — Edward Long, George Cole, John Brown and James Cummings — who had deserted their ship. They all married Native women. Cummings's bride was "Lucy," or Spukh-pu-ka-num. The couple had three daughters and two sons. One of the latter, Timothy, or "Tim," lived in Stanley Park until his death in 1958.

Effects of the 1888 smallpox epidemic were severely felt at Fishermen's Cove. Residents were not only isolated and forbidden to leave or have contact with anyone else but also the homes and outbuildings of the Gonsalveses, Sylvias, Cummings, Coles, Browns and Longs were ordered burned by the Health Inspector, along with those of a family named Smith.

One of the Smith daughters died of-the disease and became the last person buried at Brockton Point. According to descriptions at the time, her grave is near the Hallelujah Monument (12).

One of the ironies of the epidemic is that it accidentally provided historians with a very detailed record of 19th century life in Fishermen's Cove. Prior to the razing of the homes, complete lists of each family's possessions were compiled by health officials to compensate the victims. That of the Gonsalves clan alone runs to three pages and describes everything from the type and number of spoons, combs and underwear to furniture. The family estimated the value of their belongings at $700. The Health Inspector suggested $200, but when the sharp pencils at City Hall had done their work only $125 was awarded.

In forthcoming years an even more distressing experience than smallpox faced the settlers, who were actually not landowners but squatters. By definition, squatters are those who settle on land without benefit of title or purchase. This practice was quite common in 19th century Canada. Squatters were able to secure legal recognition of their property rights either by duration (proof of having occupied the land for 60 years), or through what was sometimes referred to as "historical fact." This term applied to people who had been associated with a piece of land for so long that they were considered the legitimate owners.

The situation in Stanley Park was confused. It had been set aside as a Government Reserve in 1859 but Coast Salish Natives still resided there and considered the land theirs since no treaty relinquishing title was ever signed. Pioneers settled in the future park where they wished or, in the case of many of the Fishermen's Cove residents, where Natives from the village at Lumberman's Arch said they might.

No question of this occupation was raised during the first 28 years after Fishermen's Cove was established. In 1888, however, the land that suddenly had been declared parkland was where the children of the settlers were raising the third generation. In fact, the last home to be built was in 1917 by Edward Long Junior, son of one of the 1870s shipjumpers. He asked Park authorities for permission to construct a house near where he had been born and was refused. He did so anyway.

Then, in 1921, a relatively minor incident occurred which eventually led to the death of the village. Informed that the West family rented their home to visitors as a summer cottage, Park officials began working with the City of Vancouver to evict all squatters.

The subsequent Squatter Eviction Trials were a bitter experience for people whose families had lived at Brockton Point since long before Vancouver was anything but a collection of unpainted shacks huddled on the southern shore of Burrard Inlet. But without deeds, documentation, or money to fight effectively, the conclusion was inevitable.

Despite appeals, the squatters lost their battle in 1925. Until 1931, however, they were allowed to stay in the park for a token "rent" of $1.00 a month.

After that, four of the remaining families were relocated in city tax-sale houses. In 1931 their former homes and outbuildings were

Joseph Silvia, above, also known as Portuguese Joe #1, was one of the best known of the squatters. The last squatter was Timothy "Tim" Cummings, above, who was legally blind and permitted to stay. He died in 1958.

Below: This 1880s photo shows the squatters' village at Fishermen's Cove near Brockton Point.

burned, with the exception of the West and Cummings houses. The Wests lingered for a few years, paying a monthly rent of $5. Tim Cummings, because of blindness, was allowed to live out his days in the Park, dying in 1958 at 77.

The descendants of the Brockton Point squatters today are scattered throughout British Columbia, although many of the family names have undergone changes. The Silvias became, in some cases, Silvies or Silveys; the DeCostas adopted DaCosta or DeKosta. Still, those such as Robert Cole of the Capilano Reserve or Wilfred Gonsalves of Richmond might still proudly own certificates that give as their place of birth what few can claim: "Stanley Park, Vancouver, British Columbia."

Brockton Point Cut-Off (11)
Running behind the Totem Poles from Fishermen's Cove to the Narrows, or northern shore, of Brockton Point, this brief stretch of roadway allows motorists to bypass Brockton Point Lighthouse (16) and the remainder of Brockton Point's tip.

Hallelujah Point (12)
As we reach the end of the former Fishermen's Cove, the land to the immediate left begins to rise. On this low hill is what appears to be a truncated section of wall. It is the Hallelujah Monument, erected to commemorate the Salvation Army's picnic and meeting area. The name Hallelujah Point is said to be derived from the spirited cries which carried across the harbor to Vancouver.

Pioneer Cemetery (13)
Virtually all of this rise, the park road and the wooded area beyond extending nearly to the Brockton Point Light, was Burrard Inlet's first cemetery. An estimated 200 pioneers lie here. Already in use by Coast Salish Natives for their dead when the Europeans arrived, this hillside also seemed to the latter a logical place for their cemetery.

According to descriptions at the time and later, those who died in the harbor area, including sailors from the many vessels which plied local waters, were brought by boat for burials in graves marked only with split-cedar crosses. The practice had virtually halted by 1888 when the park road was under construction, although the last recorded burial of a young girl killed by smallpox occurred that May.

The flimsy grave markers didn't endure long on the exposed slope. Unable to discern the location of most of the graves, work crews ran their roadway through the southern portions of the old cemetery. Some of the remaining crosses in the section farther back from the road where the clump of trees is today could be seen well into the 1890s. At least one photograph from this period shows

The Nine O'clock Gun and Vancouver's waterfront in 1932. The gun is still fired every night, a tradition now almost a century old. The original housing in the photo was replaced by a concrete and stone cupola in 1936, then by the present structure in 1987 to commemorate Vancouver's Centennial.

rough crosses in the undergrowth of these same woods.

Nine O'Clock Gun (14)

Officially the Time Gun, but almost invariably called the Nine O'Clock Gun, this is an electrically fired cannon which sounds at 9:00 p.m. each day. Under the right atmospheric conditions the report reputedly can be heard in Mission, some 67 km (42 miles) away.

Made of tin, antimony and copper in England in 1816, it was installed not far from its present location in 1894 after serving briefly as part of Nanaimo's defences during the Canada-U.S. boundary dispute of the mid-19th century. Myths abound about the reason for the Time Gun's presence. According to the most common, the gun signaled fishing curfew hours. Another is that it was an early timepiece for Vancouverites. The true story is far more interesting.

It began with William D. Jones, the lighthouse keeper at Brockton Point. He had repeatedly requested a cannon to end a practice he detested — firing dynamite. Captains of sailing ships in those days lived, or died, by their knowledge of tides and needed accurate time readings to gauge them. As an "aid to navigation," Jones was required to detonate a charge of dynamite at exactly 9:00 each evening so ships in port could set their chronometers. Here is Jones's account:

"We used to have a long pole just about where the new lighthouse stands now," he said in 1922, "like an exaggerated fishing rod. Instead of the regulation fishing line, it was fitted with a telegraph wire. This wire ran along it and hung down for a few feet over the water. It was my questionable privilege to bait this line with a stick of dynamite fitted with a detonator."

He carried the explosives in his jacket in inclement weather which, not surprisingly, made him wonder if there wasn't a better and safer way. His complaints about the danger resulted in the arrival of the Time Gun in 1894. Jones was quite explicit about the gun's purpose:

"It is intended for the benefit of the shipping in the harbor, to give them the benefit of correcting their chronometers once a day. The report is not the important thing either. It is the flash that counts. A ship's captain never waits for the sound to reach him. He goes by the flash."

Jones was once asked if the gun was aimed anywhere in particular. He replied that it was. It had been sighted on the City Hall of the day, squarely on the mayor's office. Asked about the potential for an accident, Jones replied: "There have been times when I considered myself the advisability of adding a good-sized rock. But I am a humane man and better thoughts prevailed."

40

First housed in a wooden structure, the Time Gun was moved to a wire-and-mesh cupola in January 1954. The current enclosure was completed in 1987 and marks the 1986 Centennial of the City of Vancouver.

HMS *Egeria* Benchmark (15)
Standing with your back to the water, you'll notice a small area partially enclosed by a chain. A plaque notes that it was used as a reference point or "benchmark" in 1898 by HMS *Egeria*, a surveying vessel. The same place was used by the Royal Engineers in 1863 during the official survey of Burrard Inlet, but the Engineers' mark had been forgotten and only rediscovered in 1936 under a covering of moss and leaves.

Brockton Point Lighthouse (16)
The first lighthouse built at Brockton Point was a wood-frame structure that went into service on September 15, 1890. Its keeper, the already mentioned William D. Jones, was hired at $300 a year. He was responsible for maintaining the fog bell and light, operating the signal masts and, from 1894 onwards, firing the Time Gun. The current lighthouse was completed in 1915.

The archway straddling the Seawall at the base of the light was originally intended to be part of a boathouse, but the treacherous currents resulted in its conversion to the span. Rusted rails on the foreshore at low tide mark where the keeper's rowboat was launched and retrieved.

Chehalis Monument (17)
Set in the fringe of trees on the far side of the road, the *Chehalis* Monument is easily overlooked from the Seawall. This flared column topped by a cross commemorates a tragic event which occurred in the waters directly opposite this point in 1906.

The Union Steamship Line's tugboat *Chehalis* had been chartered for an excursion to the oyster beds at Blunden Island. It was a warm, clear, summer's afternoon. As the *Chehalis* steered around Brockton Point to head into the Narrows, another boat was on a parallel course. Both faced into the stiff flood tide running at 8 or 9 knots.

Astern of them was the CPR ship, *Princess of Victoria*, also outward bound. The captain of the *Princess* had decided to take his faster vessel between the two boats when the *Chehalis* suddenly dropped back with the incoming tide in an attempt to reach the less turbulent eddy nearer the Stanley Park shore. The CPR captain sounded a warning but the attempt was futile. The *Chehalis's* manoeuver brought it directly under the bow of the *Princess*.

As 200 passengers looked over the rail in horror, their vessel sliced into the tug. There was an explosion of steam and the *Che-*

Brockton Point Athletic Grounds were the sports center of pioneer Vancouver.
Events were widely publicized, opposite page, and attended by thousands.
Bicycle races were a major feature of sports days, although the high-wheel bikes
shown above in 1902 had been replaced by a safer design.

Below: Brockton Point in the 1920s, the lighthouse in the foreground. Behind it
are the keeper's house and Vancouver's skyline.

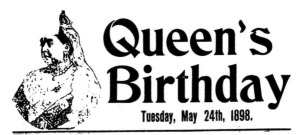

Queen's Birthday

Tuesday, May 24th, 1898.

Bicycle Races, Athletic Sports,
LACROSSE MATCH, Etc.
—AT—

Brockton Point =
(In Aid of Catholic Church Building Fund.)

Prizes have been kindly donated by His Worship
Mayor Garden and City Merchants.

SILVER CUP, donated by Mayor Garden,
For 1 Mile Amateur Bicycle Race.

FIRST-CLASS REFRESHMENTS ON GROUNDS.
BATTERY BAND
And Mission Indian Boys' Band in Attendance.
Reduced Fares from New Westminster.

⊣ PROGRAMME ⊢

10 to 12 a. m......... LACROSSE MATCH...... Intermediate.
Prize, Lacrosse Sticks and Shoes, Value $40.00.

⊣ ATHLETICS, 12 to 1.30. ⊢

1. BOYS' RACE (between 12 & 16 years), 100 yds., 1st, value $3.00, 2nd, $1.50
2. GIRLS' RACE " " " 1st, " 3.00, 2nd, 1.50
3. BOYS' RACE (under 12 years), 50 yds... ...1st, " 2.00, 2nd, 1.00
4. GIRLS' RACE " " " ... ...1st, " 2.00, 2nd, 1.00
5. QUARTER-MILE RACE, open... ...1st, " 6.00, 2nd, 3.00
6. RUNNING LONG JUMP ... ...1st, " 3.00, 2nd, 2.00
7. RUNNING HIGH JUMP ... ...1st, " 3.00, 2nd, 2.00
8. OBSTACLE RACE, 200 yds. ... ...1st, " 3.00, 2nd, 2.00
9. 100 YDS. FOOT RACE... ... ...1st, " 5.00, 2nd, 2.50
10. PUTTING 16-lb. WEIGHT ... ...1st, " 3.00, 2nd, 2.00
11. THROWING 56-lb. WEIGHT ... ...1st, " 5.00, 2nd, 2.50
12. SACK RACE, 100 yds. ... ...1st, " 3.00, 2nd, 2.00
13. MUSICAL BAND RACE, 100 yds., 1st, value 3.00. 2nd, 2.00, 3rd, 1.00

BICYCLE RACES, 2 p. m.

1. NOVICE, 1 mile ... ...1st, value $5.00, 2nd, $2.00
2. QUARTER-MILE AMATEUR, open ... ...1st, " 5.00, 2nd, 2.00
3. QUARTER-MILE PROFESSIONAL, open ...1st, cash 10.00, 2nd, 5.00
4. HALF-MILE AMATEUR, open... ... ...1st, value 5.00, 2nd, 2.50
5. ONE-MILE PROFESSIONAL, open ... ...1st, cash 10.00, 2nd, 5.00
6. ONE-MILE AMATEUR ...1st, cup, value 10.00; 2nd, value 5.00, 3rd, 2.50
7. HALF-MILE BOYS' ... ...1st, value $3.00, 2nd, $2.00
8 TWO-MILE PROFESSIONAL .. ..1st, cash 10.00, 2nd, 5.00
9. TWO-MILE AMATEUR ... ... 1st, value 7.00; 2nd, 5.00, 3rd, 2.00

NOTE.—In all races, 3 to enter or no 2nd prize, and 5 to enter or no 3rd prize.
Bicycle races held under C. W. A. rules, and under the patronage of the
Vancouver Bicycle Club, whose Officers will officiate at all races.

First-Class Lunch, 25c.
Supplied and served by the Ladies of the Congregation, from 12 noon.
Evans & Hastings, Printers.

halis immediately disappeared. The Brockton Point Lighthouse keeper hurriedly launched a boat to begin a search for survivors, as did the *Princess*.

Six of the tug's complement were rescued, but nine drowned. The dead included the recent bride of the excursion's leader, the engineer, two firemen, a cabin boy and the cook. The bereaved groom never recovered from his shock and died two years later. Subsequent court cases resulted in the CPR captain receiving a six-month suspension and the captain of the *Chehalis* exonerated but left crippled. The wreck of the *Chehalis* was never found.

In November 1906, Park authorities allowed friends of the victims to erect the *Chehalis* Monument in memory of those who had perished.

Totem Poles (18)

This vibrantly colored cluster comprises authentic Native poles from several different tribal groups, including the Haida and Kwakiutl. The figures carved on them represent a combination of characters from Native mythology and symbols of the clan, or person, responsible for their carving.

While it is popularly believed that poles were simply decorative, this belief is wrong. Some were used as corner posts inside communal homes, some were topped by a box which contained the remains of a prominent tribal member, while still others formed dramatic entrance pieces or were free-standing. The highly ritualized sculptures may tell a story by presenting the major elements of a given myth and/or describe the lineage of a particular chief or family.

Visitors are reminded that these striking examples of Native art and craftsmanship are of great historic and cultural significance. Please do not damage them.

Petroglyph Rock (19)

In the same area as the Totem Poles, Petroglyph Rock was donated by a former Parks Board chairman, W. C. "Bill" Shelley. The story of this artifact is a tribute to the generosity of one of Stanley Park's staunchest supporters.

The Rock was found in the vicinity of Lone Cabin Creek in the B.C. Interior in 1923 and brought to Vancouver in 1926 (the inscription on the plaque is inaccurate). The numerous designs incised into much of its surface are petroglyphs, wrongly called "pictographs" by the plaque's author. Petroglyphs are actual carvings, whereas pictographs are painted on the surface. They depict both real and mythological creatures.

The rock came to the attention of H.S. Brown, the so-called "Millionaire of the Cariboo," in 1923 and he informed Shelley of the find. Shelley engaged a Vancouverite named Frank Cross for the arduous task of transporting it to the coast.

It was located near the east bank of the Fraser River, approximately 80 km (50 miles) northwest of Lough Raymond Station. The immense boulder, little of which protrudes above ground at its present site, was so heavy that moving it in winter was the only feasible course.

According to Cross's notes, "...it was necessary to use the ten horses on steel double blocks ... the tremendous force would pull the logs out and we would try again and again ... heading up to get to the best place.... We nearly lost a team of horses when the rock suddenly shot ahead, going down. However, it happened to catch them in the heels and [bowled] three of them completely over the sled and the rock, like toys. They landed on their backs and apparently were not hurt at all."

After the struggle of men and animals in the middle of the Interior winter, the Petroglyph Rock was loaded aboard a train and shipped to Vancouver. The operation cost Shelley $2,000, a small fortune in the 1920s.

According to Doris Lundy, a rock art expert at the Provincial Museum in Victoria, B.C., the carvings may have been done within the past 500 years. The stone probably functioned either as a Native salmon-claim marker or was associated with tribal puberty rites. The area from which it was removed was traditionally regarded as the territory of the Shuswap Native People.

Native Canoes (20)
Facing the totem poles is a long, low shed. Until recently it housed two Native canoes, one perhaps 200 years old. They were temporarily moved to allow Native craftsmen to use the structure while carving the latest totem pole. When this book was printed, the Parks Board hadn't decided whether to reinstate the canoes or to institute a permanent carving display of Native artists.

Brockton Oval (21)
Past the Totem Poles and Petroglyph Rock a large, manicured green space appears to the left of the Seawall. This is the sports area once known as the Brockton Point Athletic Grounds but usually referred to now as Brockton Oval.

This is the land Captain Edward Stamp cleared for his ill-fated sawmill in 1865. Several months prior to the official opening of Stanley Park, this relatively unobstructed portion was already the subject of lobbying by various Vancouver sports groups desperate for a permanent athletic field.

Led by the Football Club, they made their first official request in May 1888. By September 1889 a road around the site had been completed and, in 1890, work on the grounds themselves began. In anticipation of the crowds expected, a ferry landing was built near where the Nine O'Clock Gun (14) stands.

The official opening was held over the Dominion Day weekend of July 1891 with huge crowds streaming to the Grounds. Transportation and admission was 25 cents.

The Grounds became the hub of organized sports in the Vancouver area, although not all clubs were welcome. One of the first in line was the Vancouver Rifle Association whose request for a narrow strip on the open fields for a target range was adamantly refused.

Sports Centre

By 1892 a grandstand had been added to the Grounds and the popularity of the area steadily increased. In 1913, along with golf and cycling clubs, there were the Vancouver Cricket Club, Burrard Cricket Club, Vancouver Hockey Club, Vancouver Rugby Football Union, Lawn Tennis Association, Polo and Jump Club, and the Vancouver Athletic Club. Many others used the Grounds on an occasional basis.

Demand for playing space led to extensive filling of low-lying sections in 1917 and again during the 1930s when Relief Workers completed much of the remaining grading and landscaping.

Buried Treasure?

A curious event took place during the Second World War which may have left a substantial legacy under the sports fields. In 1942, thieves robbed the Bank of Montreal at Prior and Main Streets in Vancouver and escaped with $56,500. Police were certain they knew who had committed the crime but lacked hard evidence to arrest the perpetrators.

Then, in 1945, they were approached by a woman who claimed that at least some of the loot was buried at Brockton Point. A year previous, her boyfriend had taken her to Brockton Point where he showed her where $26,000 of the loot was buried.

In her statement the woman said that the money was "...in a clearing in a clump of trees, bordering the cricket pitch at Lower Brockton Point." However, as she had visited the site only once, and at night, she couldn't relocate it. Worse, her boyfriend had been shot to death shortly after his dramatic revelation.

Although the police believed she was telling the truth, extensive digging revealed nothing. If the loot is buried at Brockton Point as the witness claimed, then it may still be there.

Today, Brockton Point has receded in importance as far as the Lower Mainland sports scene is concerned. Still, some of the best cricket and rugby teams in the world compete here on a regular basis.

Brockton Clubhouse (22)

A small concession stand for public use is on the southeast side at ground level, but no public washrooms. The nearest ones are located in the middle of the grandstand on the far side of the rugby field.

The remainder of the Brockton Clubhouse is for members only. Membership fees are quite reasonable and include use of the cosy, British-style pub on the upper floor. Views from the pub's balconies, while spectacular, can on occasion be disconcerting.

On one side a cricket match may be in progress, the players well mannered and courteous in their white uniforms. They applaud the skills of their opponents with good humor, while spectators clap their approval in a subdued fashion in keeping with a time-honored tradition of civility and decorum.

On the rugby field, however, the contest between rivals is a violent melee of testosterone run amuck. Sweat, blood and muscle-bruising, bone-snapping body-slams are routine punctuated by language most politely described as "colorful."

Girl In Wetsuit (23)

This cast bronze figure incited a fair bit of controversy when it was bolted to its stone perch in 1970. A newspaper editorial cited it as evidence that "...the silly season is just a little premature this year." and, in a parting jab, scorned it as "...a hoked-up caricature of Copenhagen's delightful little mermaid."

By contrast its sculptor, Elek Imredy, maintained that it was never intended as a more chaste version of the nubile Danish harbor sprite. It was, he said, a piece which exemplified the combination of a maritime theme with that of exploration of the sea's bounty.

Empress of Japan Figurehead (24)

This ornate and brilliantly hued dragon is the figurehead from the first *Empress of Japan.* It was presented to the Vancouver Board of Parks and Recreation in 1927 by R.W. Brown, editor of the *Province* newspaper, which also paid for its restoration in 1928.

The inscription at the time read: "Figurehead of S.S. *Empress of Japan* which plied these waters thirty-one years, 1891 to 1922, carrying Vancouver's commerce to the Orient."

The inscription was modified in 1960 to reflect the fact that the original had been replaced with a cast to protect it from further weathering. Visitors may appreciate the irony of a fire-breathing dragon facing the mountains of striking yellow sulphur heaped on the far side of Burrard Inlet.

Lumberman's Arch (25)

Although there is a Lumberman's Arch, the name is a general reference to the area as a whole which comprises a road bypass (public restrooms are contained within its curved sides), large

Lumberman's Arch was an imposing structure which reflected B.C.'s massive cedar and fir. It originally stood at Pender and Hamilton Streets in downtown Vancouver, erected in 1912 as a tribute to the visiting Duke and Duchess of Connaught. Moved to Stanley Park, it was a prominent landmark for 35 years.

concession building, waterpark and picnic ground. This popular area may be the most important archaeological site in the Park.

Part, and perhaps all, of the shoreline from the *Empress of Japan* figurehead to Lumberman's Arch and beyond — plus much of the meadow and hillsides on each side of this bowl — is the site of a large Native midden. It is also the former location of Whoi-Whoi, or XwayXway, a village of the Coast Salish people who once called Stanley Park home.

Quarrying The Past
In 1888, when the driveway which encompasses Stanley Park was being built, work crews determined that a vast deposit of broken clam shells at Lumberman's Arch provided the ideal material to surface the new road. Although they didn't appreciate the significance of what they were "mining," they were astounded by the depth and extent of what was actually an immense garbage dump created over thousands of years by the region's indigenous population. In places the shell fragments lay 2.4 m (8 feet) deep and served as the foundation for trees estimated to be up to 500 years old.

The "Indian" Lumberman's Arch
When Captain George Vancouver explored Burrard Inlet in 1792 no Native village could be seen, even though Vancouver's journal leaves no doubt that he and his crew were looking for signs of habitation that would explain the origin of the Native People who greeted him. Had there been a village at Lumberman's Arch at the time it would have been recorded.

By the 1860s, however, there definitely was a village here, noted in various accounts by travellers and others. The most likely explanation is that the site was used seasonally by Natives who lived perhaps in Howe Sound or along the Fraser River and only after 1792 were permanent dwellings built.

When pioneer John Morton arrived on July 25, 1862, he reported that some 2,000 Natives were gathered there in fear of an imminent attack by "Hydah-Kling-Gets from the north" (a reference to the Haida, one of the fiercest of the Native Peoples of the Pacific Coast whose warriors frequently conducted raiding expeditions against other Native groups).

His account was quite detailed, even noting the presence of several Natives who walked with pronounced limps. They said that they had been captives of other Indians and that each had had the cord above one knee severed to hinder escape. They had been repatriated by the British Navy as part of its continuing efforts to end slavery among the Native Peoples. Now they feared recapture.

It doesn't seem, however, that the Natives living here in the 19th century were the traditional ones to do so. In 1865 Chartres

Brew, a government official, while noting that the village was occupied by Indians, concluded that they could "...at any time be removed, the ground does not belong to their tribe."

Subsequently, a government surveyor named Launders was dispatched to map the site for Captain Edward Stamp's proposed sawmill. He noted that one corner of it "...occurs in the centre of an Indian village to clear which would give the sawmill about 90 acres (36.4 ha). By the appearance of the soil and debris this camping ground is one of the oldest in the Inlet. The resident Indians seem very distrustful of my purpose, and suspicious of encroachment on their premises...."

They had no immediate need to worry. Stamp failed in his mill-building enterprise and potlatches (celebrations) involving up to several thousand Natives and their European guests were reported into the 1880s. Then the population went into decline, quite possibly as a result of the smallpox epidemics which ravaged the Natives in the latter part of the 19th century.

The few remaining inhabitants became victims of the road surfacing project. The rather callous report of one worker states that "...the Indians were put out of their houses and we were put in. We had an excellent French cook, but the living quarters were not so good."

As they dug into the midden, he and his fellows discovered one skeleton after another. Famed archaeologist Charles Hill-Tout visited the excavations on several occasions and interviewed those who had worked on it. Hill wrote that:

"They opened one of the later or Salish middens, utilizing the material for the road.... A considerable number of skeletons was disinterred from the midden mass ... the larger bones and crania of which were gathered up and placed in boxes which were afterwards hidden in the forest where I discovered them a few years later. The crania had then fallen to pieces ... it would seem that burial by inhumation sometimes took place in former times even by the Squamish themselves, though this was not the prevailing custom when we first came into contact with them."

During the smallpox epidemic of 1888-90 the houses were slated for burning. This may have been when a central lodge called "Tay Hay" was razed as there is no further reference to it. But at least some of the other buildings survived. In December 1899, the Parks Superintendent reported that two of three remaining Indian houses were vacant. By October 1900 these had been bought by authorities for $25 each and burned.

The last vestige of XwayXway was the home of Aunt Sally, an elderly Native woman. As already mentioned, during the Squatter Eviction Trials of the 1920s she was the only Stanley Park resident able to establish a legal right to live there. Her property was purchased for $15,500 by W.C. "Bill" Shelley, the same philanthropist who gifted the park with the Petroglyph Rock. He was later reimbursed by the Federal Government, although grudgingly.

Village To Park
In 1905 a deer paddock was built and in 1911 a broad, sweeping roadway constructed between what is now the Aquarium (see Walk II) and the main park driveway near where Aunt Sally's house still stood.

(Called the Esplanade, it was later torn up and the roadbed replaced with grass — but its location is still evident. The two rows of deciduous trees which curve down from the Aquarium through the picnic area almost to the pedestrian underpass were originally planted on the sides of the Esplanade.)

The feature that gave this section its name was the next arrival — an enormous rustic structure known as the Lumberman's Arch, erected in 1913. It was donated by the Lumberman's and Shingleman's Society.

Although officially renamed the Bowie Arch in honor of its designer, George Bowie who was killed at Ypres during World War One, Lumberman's Arch was too entrenched in popular reference. Lumberman's Arch it remains to this day. The massive original span stood until 1947 when for safety reasons it was replaced with the present more modest one.

By 1920, Lumberman's Arch looked like a miniature zoo, with animal collections including deer, goats and elk, the latter moved from their original site where the Lawn Bowling Greens (44) are today.

The Seawall reached Lumberman's Arch in 1926. A saltwater swimming pool was added in 1932 but, considered a liability, was converted into the Variety Kids' Park in 1986.

Lumberman's Arch Today
Its Native past, too, still makes its presence felt. Human remains were found in 1928 and 1962, while portions of the old midden have recently been exposed by foot traffic at the north side of the food concession building.

Unfortunately, Lumberman's Arch is probably one of the least attractive areas in the entire park. The problem is litter which is everywhere, especially on weekends and holidays.

While some of the blame can be attributed to slovenly park patrons, the major cause is the outdated and too few trash containers. Of the open-top variety in many cases, they're easy prey for foraging crows, raccoons and seagulls which industriously spread the contents far and wide.

Beaver Lake Creek and Beaver Lake (26)(27)
Beaver Lake Creek, which exits under the Seawall and is marked

The *Beaver,* above, was the
first steam vessel on the
Pacific Coast of both North
and South America. For
over 50 years — from fur
trade days to the railway
era — she plied B.C.
waters. In 1888 her long
years of service ended
when she ran aground on
Calamity Point.

Prospect Point Lighthouse in the 1920s. The stairs to the left of the Lighthouse led to Signal Station, shown below on opening day in July 1923. The Station has disappeared, its legacy a series of terraces which are popular viewpoints.

by a stone-faced archway to the left, is the next point of interest on the Seawall Walk. This creek drains Beaver Lake (27) which lies only 300 m (some 330 yards) upstream and is easily reached by a path which follows the creek through a narrow band of forest. (See Walk III for more details on Beaver Lake.)

In recent years the creek has become a spawning area for salmon after wild stocks had been reported absent for many decades. However, their continued viability is uncertain. Due to the stream's size and shallow depth, salmon eggs buried in the fine gravels of the bed are quite vulnerable. Riding bicycles — mountain bike owners seem to be the chief offenders — or wading through Beaver Lake Creek will destroy eggs. Please be considerate and refrain from doing either.

Chaythoos (28)

Although there isn't anything on the Seawall or Park maps to indicate it, Chaythoos (a Native name meaning a high bank or place) is important to Stanley Park's history.

As you continue along the Seawall from the arch over Beaver Lake Creek you'll notice a fairly large cleared area to your left. There's a grassy embankment with a trail leading to it from the Seawall and on top are park benches, a covered signboard and a plaque (not visible from below) announcing the re-dedication of Stanley Park in 1988.

This is the same site where the park was dedicated by Lord Stanley on October 29, 1889. It is also the former dwelling place of two well-known members of Vancouver's Native community. Jack Khatsahlano and his son, August Jack, had their home here. The main houses, some small outbuildings and two above-ground tombs on stilts appear on official sketches made when the park road was being planned. Considered a hindrance to the driveway, all but the two funeral houses were demolished. The human remains in the latter were eventually sent to Squamish for burial.

In 1889, Vancouver began receiving water from the Capilano River on the north shore of Burrard Inlet. Pipes were laid on the bottom of the Narrows and through Stanley Park along what is now called Pipeline Road. In 1894 a home was built at Chaythoos by the Water Works caretaker, Frank Harris, to house a family which eventually included 10 children. Many of the shrubs still growing in that portion of Chaythoos today were part of the Harris garden.

Prospect Point (29)

Over the years, Prospect Point has been shown on maps and charts as Calamity Point, South Head, Observation Point and Prospect Bluff. It is the highest feature of Stanley Park, rearing some 64.3 m (211 feet) above the sea. Its perpendicular wall of volcanic columns caused by the sea cooling the outer edge of the ancient lava flow stands like half of a ruined portal marking the entrance to Burrard Inlet.

In Native legend there are caves deep within the stone of Prospect Point which cannot be entered by mortals from land or water. In one of these dwells Si'Atmulth — the Rainmaker. According to legend, Si'Atmulth lived with his wife and son in a lodge at the top of what we now call Prospect Point.

When the Rainmaker pushed aside the skin that covered his doorway, rain fell on the earth. When he closed the flap, the rain stopped. In this way the Rainmaker controlled the growth of all living things.

But there came a day when the Rainmaker, angered by the People's lack of respect for his work and gifts, pulled the skin tightly across the doorway and refused to open it. At first this was not noticed by the People, but after a time the grass began to turn brown, the trees withered and, one by one, the streams and lakes became dry as dust.

Finally, one tribe decided to send two of its bravest warriors to the Rainmaker's lodge.

When they arrived, they discovered that they could not enter through the front door flap so they crept down through the smoke-hole in the roof, dropping to the cavern floor far below. There they seized Si'Atmulth's son and, being careful not to wake his sleeping parents, undid the door flap and fled with their young captive.

The Rainmaker awoke and discovered that the door was open; outside, rain fell steadily. Realizing what had happened, he went to the tribe and asked for the return of his son, promising that if they were reunited he would never withhold the rain again. The People agreed to the bargain.

From that day to this, although sometimes it may not rain for a long while, the Rainmaker has always kept his promise.

Lions Gate Bridge (30)
In June 1909, the Parks Board was approached by the Burrard Wire Cable Bridge Company with a proposal to erect a bridge at Prospect Point "somewhat after the pattern of the Eiffel Tower." The attempt was rebuffed by Park officials aghast at the idea of an access road to the bridge through Stanley Park.

Then in 1926 a delegation representing British interests again raised the subject. The Parks Board left the decision to Vancouverites. In a public plebiscite the following year they overwhelmingly rejected the project which would have effectively cut Stanley Park in two.

But in 1933 another British scheme for the First Narrows crossing was approved because of severe unemployment caused by the

Great Depression. Only one Parks Commissioner, E.G. Baynes, stood against the partitioning of the park by a massive bridge and a 2.4 km (1.5 mile) access road, plus approaches.

It was the worst blow ever to befall Stanley Park. The access road cut through its very heart, severing trails dating back to the old skid roads of early loggers. The most isolated and undeveloped regions of the forest were suddenly carved open.

Promoted as a solution to unemployment, the bridge would primarily benefit British developers, including the Guinness family of brewing fame. They had assembled a massive tract of raw land stretching across West Vancouver on the North Shore of Burrard Inlet to Horseshoe Bay.

Ironically, the lights which are strung across Lions Gate Bridge today are a recent "beautification" gift from the Guinnesses whose family had been so instrumental in bisecting Stanley Park.

Sunz (31)

Near Prospect Point Lighthouse, and easily overlooked, is a misshapen lump of sandstone on the immediate foreshore that stands almost even with the rim of the Seawall. Known in Native lore as "Sunz," this is a woman who features in two conflicting legends.

According to one version, she is the wife of the warrior who became Siwash Rock (35) as a form of reward. In the other, it is said that while washing her hair she was turned to stone by the gods as punishment for some unspecified affrontery.

At any rate, the Seawall construction carefully curved around Sunz to ensure that she was left undisturbed, thanks to the intervention of City Archivist Major Matthews. However, wave erosion and vandalism have been damaging and Sunz may soon succumb to the sea and ignorant behavior.

Prospect Point Lighthouse (32)

The reason for a beacon here is the shipwreck of the S.S. *Beaver*, the first steamship to ply the entire West Coast of North America. Built for the Hudson's Bay Company in England in 1835, she was 31 m (101-feet) long with a crew of 26 and five small cannons.

Vancouver City Council first requested a warning device at Prospect Point in February 1888. Nothing happened, then on July 26 concern turned to outrage when the *Beaver*, now the most famous vessel on the B.C. coast, ran aground at "Calamity Point," tearing a gaping hole in her side.

It should have been an easy matter to lift the *Beaver* off the rocks but a shortage of barges to float the vessel effectively doomed her. Over the next few months she was battered by tide and wave until she slipped off the rocks and sank.

Despite the disaster, not until October 1, 1898, ten years later, did a light go into operation. The first lighthouse was a square wooden affair with a lantern at the middle of the roof and a bell in a projecting gable at the front.

The next development at Prospect Point was on the summit. In 1891 a small area was cleared to accommodate a rustic gazebo, complete with thatched roof.

At the same time, the main park road was being rerouted. The original approach to the bluff had been deemed too steep and was replaced with the one in use today. The obsolete section was relegated to the status of park trail and so it remains. Marked by sawn-off logs imbedded at its entrance, the trail begins just across the park driveway from the Seawall at Chaythoos.

Then, in 1909, a much larger project was undertaken on the bluff, one that explains the series of stone terraces so popular with visitors. A semaphore, or signal, station was constructed by the Department of Marine and Fisheries to direct ship traffic into and out of Burrard Inlet. It served as a valuable navigational aid until 1939. Then the buildings were removed, but the open terraces remained to provide an ideal vantage point for views of the North Shore Mountains, Lions Gate Bridge and English Bay.

Other changes to the upper reaches of Prospect Point have included the disappearance of the 1930s-era barbeque stand in favor of a proper restaurant (33) with take-out and public washroom facilities, a small but beautifully tended ornamental garden and a cairn commemorating the wreck of the *Beaver*.

In addition, Prospect Point is home to a large seabird colony (34). Pelagic cormorants predominate but several other species also nest, building their precarious homes on basaltic outcrops and in shallow niches.

There are approximately 60 nesting pairs of the large, black cormorants in the colony, the appetites of their young ensuring a constant influx and efflux of harried adults. Since the sun can be punishing on the exposed cliff for junior family members, the adults standing with wings outspread are probably not drying their feathers but providing protection for the hatchlings.

The cormorants share their lofty perches with several pairs of pigeon guillemots and glaucous-winged gulls. The former, seemingly one of nature's jokes with their stocky bodies and pigeon-like heads, are the colony's least noticeable inhabitants given their preference for deep crevices where their nests are hidden from view.

Two other species of cormorant can occasionally be found here and in the immediate area: the Brandt's, which prefer to perch on Siwash Rock (35) and are distinguished by a bright yellow slash at the base of their beaks, and the double-crested.

Western Seawall

The pungent aroma of the seabird colony mercifully fading, visi-

Two fallers on their springboards confront a towering Western Red Cedar. As noted on page 94, springboard holes still can be seen on stumps in Stanley Park.

58

tors now find themselves approaching the wilder, less-developed region of the Stanley Park marine boundary. Sea-sculpted walls of fern-draped sandstone are now a constant buttress on the Seawall's left side and the waves of English Bay frequently crash violently against, and even onto, the Seawall pathway.

Visitors to this portion of the Seawall are cautioned that sections of the soft sandstone cliffs do fall onto the pathway. Although the cliffs are carefully monitored, keep alert in this area.

Siwash Rock (35)

Why this distinctive, 15.2-m (50-foot) pinnacle of eroded lava dyke is called Siwash Rock is uncertain. On Admiralty Charts of 1864 it is designated "Nine Pin Rock" and, with its bulbous base, it does resemble a bowling pin. But from approximately 1884 onwards Siwash Rock has been used without exception.

The word Siwash is believed by some to be a corruption of the French "sauvage" (wild) or the English "savage." Others, including the 19th century missionary Charles Tate, who was something of an expert on Native languages and dialects, stated that it should properly have been pronounced "Slay-kay-ulsh," from the Squamish word for "He-is-standing-up," and that pioneers distorted it.

At any rate, the brooding, solitary monolith is central to several versions of Native legends. One is "Siwash the Unselfish":

"Long ago, a Squamish warrior and his tribe heard that Q'uas the Transformer had been sent on a mission to visit every People in the world, hearing and perhaps granting wishes to those with favours to ask.

"When Q'uas was said to be approaching his village, Skalsh, or Slah-kay-ulsh as some believe he was called, went for a long swim in English Bay to purify himself for the anticipated meeting. As he was doing so, he eventually noticed a canoe in the distance and swam over to greet the occupants.

"Asked why he was swimming, he told the visitors that Q'uas the Transformer was due shortly and that he wished to purify himself beforehand to be worthy to meet him.

"One of the passengers in the canoe said that he assumed this to mean that Skalsh had a personal request to make of Q'uas. But Skalsh replied that he sought nothing for himself, only aid for his tribe. The passenger persisted, asking him again if there wasn't something he wanted for himself. Skalsh reiterated that his only concern was for those of his village.

"On hearing this second denial, the passenger revealed that he was in fact Q'uas the Transformer and that of all the people he had met throughout the world, only Skalsh had been unselfish. So impressed was he with the warrior that he transformed Skalsh into the rocky pinnacle to remind all people for all time of how the spirits wished the People to be.

"So to this day, Skalsh the Unselfish stands on the shore of Stanley Park as an example to all who see him."

Siwash Rock was the home for several years of an escapee from the Stanley Park Zoo: Russell, the mountain goat.

Rescued by a fisherman in Bute Inlet when he was still quite young, Russell was brought to Steveston and picked up by then-Curator of the Stanley Park Zoo, Larry LeSage. He placed the complacent and presumably injured goat on the back seat of his car and set off for Vancouver. The little white bundle on the rear seat didn't move — at least not until LeSage stopped for a red light at the busy intersection of Granville and Broadway streets in Vancouver.

Russell suddenly leaped out an open window and bounded down Broadway. Weaving along on foot in his erratic wake was LeSage, desperately dodging drivers startled by the sight of a chuffing man trying desperately to keep up with the energetic youngster.

Although finally captured and safely housed in the zoo, Russell evidently remembered his earlier success at evasion. One spring day in 1966, he sprang over the fence of his pen and disappeared into the depths of Stanley Park. Over the next few days zoo staff found his tracks in various locations around the park but no goat. Eventually, he was discovered nibbling greenery on the cliffs around Siwash Rock.

As there was no safe way to bring him down, Russell was left alone for the better part of a year. Then Russell discovered that car roofs and hoods made ideal springboards. He took to romping across vistors' vehicles parked at Prospect Point, delightedly bouncing from car to car to the annoyance of the owners and the great amusement of passersby.

Despite staff sorties, Russell left tiny hoofprint-shaped dents in one automobile after another. Then, predictably, a car put a fatal dent in him when he landed directly in front of it.

Fort Siwash (36)

Above Siwash Rock is a World War Two searchlight emplacement that formed part of Vancouver's defences. This was also the site of an artillery battery in World War One. (See Walk IV for more details.)

Just after World War Two in this area patrolling Park police made an unusual arrest. A man named John Hood was surprised by the officers "...brewing tea in the doorway of a cave near Siwash Rock."

Hood told police that he was fond of the spot because unsuspecting nude sunbathers frequented the limited nearby beach area.

He also said that the cave wasn't his but "belonged" to another illegal park resident, "Frenchie" Wilfred Chicoine who was subsequently arrested.

Charged with vagrancy, Frenchie appeared in court where he revealed to the presiding judge that he had lived in Stanley Park for 17 years, leaving only to fight in the Second World War. A police witness, impressed by the hermit's unorthodox dwelling, testified on his behalf that "the cave was neat and clean."

The tidy war veteran was given the choice of finding a new home outside the Park, or being assigned one by the judge for a minimum of one year.

Third Beach (37)

Third Beach is, in its current form at any rate, quite recent. It was largely a mass of seaweed-covered boulders when the Parks Board dug a well in 1905. They then more or less ignored the bay until 1928 when dressing rooms and toilet facilities were added, followed by a concession stand in 1935.

The beach and shoreline extending as far as Ferguson Point (39) were closed to the public during World War Two when they were taken over by the military. Barracks were erected at Third Beach, barbed wire was strung along the access paths and foreshore, and the area became part of a defensive ring drawn around English Bay.

The Parks Board and military authorities waged their own little war over control of the beach, the former continually sniping at the latter for such things as unpaid concession accounts (totalling $11.90), the value of the beach to "public morale" and the Board's undisguised view that occupation of its property was unlikely to deter anyone, let alone marauding German or Japanese battleships.

The last wartime "contribution" of Third Beach occurred during the summer of 1944 when 300 CWAC's (Canadian Women's Army Corps) used the site as a training zone. They began arriving in July at what, due to censorship restrictions, was enigmatically described as being "...near a former army camp at a beach in Stanley Park." The fact that squads of salivating newspaper cameramen were swarming over the beach for pictures of warriors in bathing suits made this one of the worst-kept secrets of the Second World War.

In 1955, a young archaeologist named Don Abbott conducted a limited exploration at Third Beach. Although unable to properly excavate the area, he determined that the bay had been an important location for Native food gatherers. The midden he discovered was, by his calculations, originally three times the size of the one at Lumberman's Arch.

The beach proper was finally created in 1962 when 76,453 cubic meters (100,000 cubic yards) of sand were pumped from around Siwash Rock onto the stony foundation of Third Beach. Today, Third Beach has a large parking lot, concession stand, lifeguard station, public washrooms and picnic area.

One of the cleanest and quietest of the city's beaches, it offers bathers an opportunity to see bald eagles wheeling overhead, blue herons stalking the shoreline, seals bobbing just offshore and the occasional porpoise breaking the surface of English Bay. On most days, the mountain peaks of Vancouver Island appear as a dark blue line on the western horizon, a dramatic backdrop for the freighters from around the world which anchor waiting their turn to enter the Port of Vancouver.

Ferguson Point (39)
From Third Beach, the Seawall begins a pronounced curve seaward to skirt a low headland — Ferguson Point — and a panorama of English Bay, Vancouver Island, the western shore of Stanley Park and a good portion of Vancouver itself. A steep path just around the tip of the point leads to this viewpoint.

Named for A.G. Ferguson, an American who became one of the Parks Board's early Commissioners, Ferguson Point became the final resting place of famed Native poet Pauline Johnson.

Following her death in 1913, officials honored Johnson's request to be buried somewhere in the park she had loved, and a site on the northern side of Ferguson Point was chosen. Her grave is marked by a memorial fountain and cairn, while a plaque records her roots in the Iroquois Six Nations of southern Ontario and her Native name, Tekahionwake. (To learn more about Johnson, see Walk V.)

Ferguson Point: The War Years
Preparations for World War Two began early at Ferguson Point with notification of the Parks Board in January 1938, that fortifications would be built immediately. The park road was realigned and plans made to build two gun emplacements, several barrack-style structures and an underground magazine. Civic groups and Parks officials protested but to no avail. Ferguson Point was officially part of the coast defences.

A few months later these criticisms cooled when the Japanese seized two Aleutian Islands and an American freighter was torpedoed at the mouth of the Strait of Juan de Fuca. In addition, on June 20, 1942, a submarine surfaced off Estevan Lighthouse on Northern Vancouver Island and lobbed several shells at it.

Naval guns and searchlights were installed but by September 1943, the panic had largely subsided and the battery was no longer fully manned.

Ferguson Point Today
Two park benches on the center of the roughly triangular lawn sit

on one of the gun positions. As well, the entire underground magazine and elevator mechanism used to raise shells from the bunkers to the guns is still intact, although badly flooded. The rectangular metal plate on the eastern base of the grass beside the road covers the entryway.

Ferguson Point Teahouse (40), one of Vancouver's more popular restaurants, is actually the former officers' quarters and the only surviving military building on the site, although modified beyond recognition.

Second Beach (41)

One of the principal attractions here may no longer exist by the time this book is printed. The outdoor pool (42) which has served untold thousands of bathers during its 60-year history may be eliminated. Other features, however, will continue to draw visitors. These include the Ceperley Playground (43), playing fields, a large picnic area at the south end, washroom and food concession facilities and the beach itself.

Second Beach, as is the case with all of Stanley Park, has a rich and sometimes humorous past. This western shore of the park was noted by the Spanish explorer, Galiano, and his English counterpart, George Vancouver, in 1792. Both men seem to have believed that Second Beach was not dry land but water since their maps depicted Stanley Park as an island separated from the remainder of Burrard Peninsula.

Technically, they may have been right. Donald Burton, a Vancouver resident born just after the beginning of the 20th century, recalled having completely circumnavigated the park in a canoe without having to portage.

He and many other residents and visitors paddled into what is now Lost Lagoon and a freshwater lake but which was then simply the shallow upper head of Coal Harbour. (Lost Lagoon is not a natural lake but one created by closing off the western end with the causeway on which the north end of Georgia Street is built.)

Once at the extreme western side of Coal Harbour, Burton simply pointed the prow of his canoe into the creek which still exists and followed it to its exit on English Bay. From there he was able to continue his journey around the park back to Coal Harbour.

What Galiano and Vancouver based their maps on was probably not the creek alone but the wet marshy area at its mouth. Since 1914 when some 500 truckloads of material were hauled to the site, officials have been steadily adding fill to the area.

The first printed reference to Second Beach was its identification as a campground for miners heading to the Fraser River during the 1858 gold rush. During the summer some 30,000 hopeful fortune hunters arrived in Victoria and many stayed at Second

Stanley Park's massive trees have fascinated visitors for over a century.

Beach on their way to the gold-laden river bars.

They weren't the first to stop here though. The Native name was "Stait-Wouk" which is said to translate to "white clay." The name is a reference to the fired color of the blue-grey clay which lined the former creek. It was used as a whitener and for making pipes, apparently of sufficient importance to attract canoe-borne Natives from as far away as Vancouver Island long before the first Europeans settled nearby.

Of Fish Heads and Morals

Bathing sheds and firepits were built at Second Beach in 1904 but the waterfront must have been far from ideal for swimming. The Parks Superintendent complained in 1905 that he didn't have the manpower to keep the shore free of offal — fish heads, guts and other rotting debris — swept into English Bay from the Fraser River canneries.

Nevertheless, in 1906 Second Beach attire came under fire with indignant complaints from the Vancouver Morals Society about the shocking one-piece bathing suits. And this at a time when "one-piece" denoted a suit that covered the wearer from chin to ankles.

Following the cutting of a trail from here to Prospect Point in 1912, and the construction of a fully equipped bathhouse, the beach rapidly became one of the city's favorites. The shoreline was hand-cleared of rocks and sand pumped onto it to create a beach.

The first section of the Seawall in the Park was built here in 1917, in part by work gangs from the city jail, beginning the pathway which today virtually encircles the Park.

The Ceperley Playground, named for the benefactor who bequeathed her estate to the Parks Board in 1918, also benefited from labor crews supplied by the police. They cleared much of the brush from the rear of the beach area for the play site.

The now-doomed swimming pool opened amid much fanfare in 1932 — and another assault on morals. Next year men were being arrested for appearing topless on the beach. Sensitive to the public outcry against this reckless display of male flesh, Parks Board beach regulations were posted in 1934 prohibiting "...men's trunks not of sufficient height to cover the navel."

Just to be safe, the Board also banned skin-colored suits for both sexes in case anyone thought the wearer was nude.

The next challenge came in 1946 when a syndicate petitioned officials for permission to use the swimming pool as a holding tank for a sea monster they intended to ensnare. The group claimed that it was confident that it could locate and capture "Caddy the Sea Serpent," a legendary marine creature that is the West Coast's counterpart to Loch Ness in Scotland.

Before the Parks Board could enact a new regulation outlawing mythical wildlife, the syndicate reported failure and saved them the trouble. But more trouble was coming — and from within.

In 1948 one of their fellow Parks Commissioners, Rowe Holland, suggested that Second Beach was an ideal location for nude sunbathing. He had been convinced by the Canadian Sunbathing Association that doffing one's duds would reduce colds, catarrh, sinus and other complaints "...directly attributable to a lack of sunshine and fresh air in modern life."

Dismayed, the other Commissioners speedily amended beach rules to exclude nudity, prompting one newspaper editorial writer to opine that "It was decided the sun might be the undoing of some but there would be no undoing in Vancouver sunshine."

But there was undoing — sun or no sun. Within days, police issued summonses for six men found bathing in the buff at Second Beach. Each of the courageous skinnydippers was fined $10.

Before the frolicking freedom fighters could reassert their right to bare arms — and everything else — the fresh air affair was rendered moot by exposure fears of a more pressing kind. Catastrophic flooding in the Fraser Valley forced the closure of all city beaches to reduce the possibility of a typhoid epidemic.

Another interesting aspect of the Ceperley Playground is where it borders the picnic area. There is a low stone wall delineating the two made up of what are, for the most part, rough-hewn granite slabs. Quite a few of these slabs are far smoother and symmetrical than others and for good reason — they're mortuary pieces.

In 1968, base and name stones from the 1919 section of Mountainview Cemetery were trucked to the play area and incorporated in the divider. All, however, were stones in need of replacement. They weren't simply plucked out of the graveyard. All names and other identifying features have been faced into the hill or downwards to avoid any misunderstanding, but it is obvious which ones originated in the cemetery.

The Ceperley Playground is almost the end of the Seawall Walk, with Beach Avenue entrance/exit only some 500 m away (approx. 550 yards).

There are, however, quite a few facilities packed into this last stretch, all to the left of the Seawall.

Lawn Bowling (44)
The Lawn Bowling greens are located just inside Stanley Park and may be the first feature visitors entering from this direction notice after the offices of the Vancouver Board of Parks and Recreation (50) known informally as the Parks Board.

Since the site was initially cleared for an elk paddock, when lawn bowlers began playing in 1919 their first green was still bounded by fencing on one side.

Although long considered a sport for the elderly, at least in Vancouver, lawn bowling is gaining popularity among younger players. It's not a difficult game to understand and the bowlers themselves are an approachable lot quite willing to field enquiries from the interested.

Sports Pavilion (45)
Just northeast of the Lawn Bowling Greens is the Sports Pavilion. Originally intended as a service center for the various sports facilities in the immediate area, the Sports Pavilion is now primarily a private restaurant which operates under lease from the Parks Board.

In recent years the Sports Pavilion has been identified by the public according to whatever name the eatery advertises, a designation which can cause some confusion as there have been a few. At the time of this writing, for example, visitors may be told that this is the Beach House (the previous incarnation) or the Fish House (the current one).

Putting Greens (46) and Pitch-And-Putt (47)
The small Putting Greens (46) in front of the Fish House/Sports Pavilion are open to the public. A kiosk on the site has the necessary equipment.

To the east of the Sports Pavilion is an 18-hole, scaled-down golf course (47) which is also open to the public with a fee structure based on the player's age. Designed by professional golf architects Walker and McPherson in 1932, the course is a beautifully landscaped one that is quite genteel and garden-like. Large West Coast trees of various species dot the miniature fairways, adding some interesting hazards.

Tennis Courts (48)
The Sports Pavilion area has several tennis courts, complemented by a smaller number on the south side of Lost Lagoon. (See Walk V for the latter.) Most of the courts are free and there is no dress code to worry about. The only limitations are those which occasionally occur when championships are scheduled.

Tennis is one of the more popular sports played in the Park but it has also been the center of some controversy over the years. Lawn tennis courts had been set up at Brockton Point just after the turn of the century. Hard-surfaced courts didn't arrive in the park until 1929 but by 1934 there were 11 in use, most near the Sports Pavilion. Yet there were problems of an unusual sort, at least from our modern viewpoint, almost from the beginning.

According to the Lord's Day Act, the courts were closed on Sundays, resulting in conflict between those who wanted to play and those who didn't want them to. The Parks Board bowed to the

The southern approach to Lions Gate Bridge cut through the heart of Stanley Park. When the bridge was proposed in 1927, it was overwhelmingly rejected in a plebiscite. In 1933, however, Parks Commissioners approved the project.

The Indian village of Xway-Xway and Lumberman's Arch in 1913. At the site a midden of seashells eight feet deep indicated that Indians had lived here for thousands of years.

righteous opposition's insistence that the former enforce its own regulations. In 1912 the Parks Superintendent was required to padlock the courts.

Tennis advocates and the clergy (backed by such groups as the Vancouver Morals Society) rallied continually over the next 20 years until finally sin won out over soul and the Sunday prohibition ended.

By "coincidence" the regulations were lifted in 1932, the same year that the golf course opened, a pet project of one of the Parks Commissioners. At the risk of an atrocious pun, no link between the two has ever been established.

Just behind the tennis courts is the Shuffleboard Court (49).

We have now reached the end of the Seawall Walk. The first building visitors see when entering Stanley Park on the English Bay side and the last when leaving it is the headquarters of the Vancouver Board of Parks and Recreation at 2099 Beach Avenue (50). For information call 681-1141.

While the Seawall is the longest and most popular of the Park's routes, it is only one of many. Visitors can enjoy a part or parts of its length and branch off onto one of the interior trails. For those who find the entire Seawall a bit daunting, look for some of the key cut-offs such as the one that runs from Coal Harbour north to Burrard Inlet at Lumberman's Arch via the zoo and aquarium (see Walk II).

ONE FINAL NOTE: If you decide to hike the interior paths, remember that the northwest portions, especially around Prospect Point, are densely forested. There are few signs to mark routes and disorientation is possible. All trails, however, eventually lead to some identifiable feature such as a road, beach and so on. So you're never really lost — just temporarily misplaced.

The refreshment pavilion in 1929. Blue jeans and sweat shirts obviously
were not considered proper attire.

STANLEY PARK WALKS: II

THE ENTERTAINMENT LOOP

This is the peanuts-and-popcorn circuit, a relatively short walk of
only 2.7 km (1.6 miles.)

It includes the Stanley Park Zoo where "wildlife" sometimes refers to the pro- and anti-zoo forces constantly vying for supremacy,
the Vancouver Public Aquarium which displays more live specimens than any other similar facility in North America; the children's, or petting, zoo; Stanley Park Pavilion; Malkin Bowl;
Miniature Railway and the Rose Gardens.

If you're feeling gregarious, this is the walk for you. Sooner or
later most Stanley Park visitors stroll through here: over 1.2 million
to the main zoo alone each year, another 700,000 to the Miniature
Railway and 800,000 to the world-class aquarium.

Because many of these folks visit during June, July and August
there's a problem. There simply aren't enough parking slots in the
Park to accommodate every car — well over 7,000,000 a year at last
count plus some 200-250 tour buses a day. That's why the Entertainment Loop Walk begins at the Georgia Street entrance (1) to
Stanley Park and assumes that the reader is on foot. You can, however, start this walk at any point, one of the nice things about
loops.

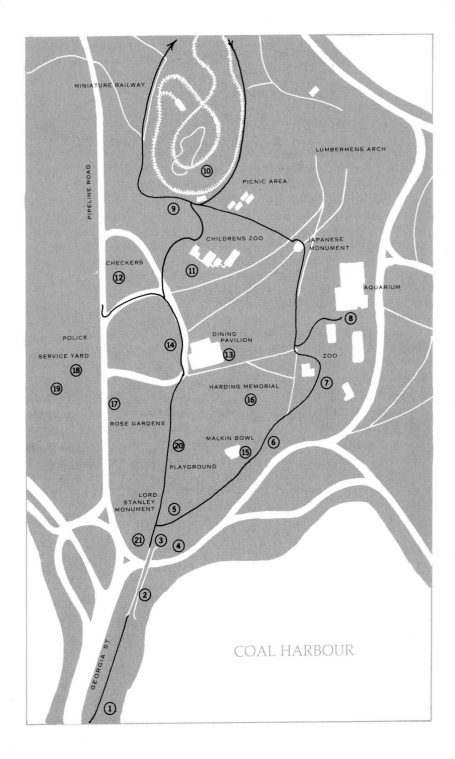

MINIATURE RAILWAY

PIPELINE ROAD

LUMBERMENS ARCH

PICNIC AREA

⑩

⑨

CHILDRENS ZOO

JAPANESE MONUMENT

CHECKERS

⑫

⑪

AQUARIUM

POLICE

SERVICE YARD

⑱

⑲

⑰

ROSE GARDENS

⑭

DINING PAVILION

⑬

ZOO

⑧

⑦

HARDING MEMORIAL

⑯

⑳

MALKIN BOWL

⑮

⑥

PLAYGROUND

LORD STANLEY MONUMENT

⑤

㉑ ③ ④

②

GEORGIA ST

①

COAL HARBOUR

For those who felt adventurous and brought a vehicle and actually found somewhere to park, consult the map at the beginning of this chapter then locate the nearest numbered feature to where you are. Those who brought a car and didn't find parking needn't despair. Many of the sights mentioned on this walk can be glimpsed from your vehicle. By the fifth or eighteenth time you pass them you'll feel quite at home.

The Entertainment Loop — 2.7 km (1.6 miles)
This Walk begins on the east side of Georgia Street (1) at the Stanley Park boundary. You have two choices: bear right, in which case you'll be on the Seawall, or go straight ahead onto what appears to be a broad concrete pedestrian bridge with ivy-covered railings and quaint lampposts called the Promenade (2).

If you bear right, refer to Walk I because you made the wrong choice and none of the following directions will make the slightest sense.

The Promenade (2)
Sometimes also called the Boulevard in older Parks Board tourist material, the Promenade was designed in 1925 by sculptor Charles Marega who also has to his credit the Harding Memorial (16), the lions at the south end of the Lions Gate Bridge and the Burrard Bridge.

Marega suggested the "grand central boulevard" rather than the proposed tunnel under consideration at the time by park officials. Anyone who has ever spent time in tunnels can understand that Marega's alternative has added immeasurably to an appreciation of the sweeping views from this vantage point of Coal Harbour to the right and Lost Lagoon on the left.

Just before the end of the Promenade there are a statue and a monument. The closer of these (3) is a towering salute to that famous son of Scotland, Robbie Burns, unofficial patron saint of poets and sheep innards. It was erected in 1928 through the efforts of the Vancouver Burns Fellowship.

On the far side is a memorial (4), often unnoticed because it sits well away from the Promenade and can't be seen from the Seawall. This is the Queen Victoria monument, erected in 1905 "by the school children of Vancouver."

At the extreme northern end of the Promenade is yet another statue (5), this one of a jolly-looking gent with arms upraised as if either warding off the legions of incontinent pigeons and seagulls or signifying surrender. The statue depicts Lord Stanley dedicating the park named in his honor.

The former Governor-General of Canada (1888-1893) wasn't Vancouver's first choice to dedicate the Park although records of that October 26, 1889, indicate that no one was boorish enough to mention the fact. Lord Strathcona was to have been immortalized but he apparently suggested Stanley in his stead. Perhaps someone had warned him about the size and productivity of the local bird population.

At any rate, what was very nearly "Strathcona Park" became "Stanley Park."

One final note is that Lord Stanley's statue stands atop the former bear pit, the main attraction of the Park's first zoo. More about that later.

Stanley's statue marks a crossroads. Straight ahead is a small playground (20); a branch to the right leads past the rear of Malkin Bowl (15) and enters the main zoo (7) via an artists' colony of sorts (6) where amateurs and professionals rub easels with democratic abandon.

The open air art studio and emporium is itself squeezed onto the grassy area that divides the Stanley Park Zoo parking lot from the zoo itself. It inspires occasional jousts in the letters-to-the-editor columns of local newspapers where critics debate the relative merits of the wares displayed. A fair comment would be that the good news is that some of the artwork is for sale; the bad news is that some of the artwork is for sale.

Stanley Park Zoo (7)
This isn't one central facility but several. The main portion, or Lower Zoo, is the where we are now. Visitors should be aware, however, that there is also a Children's Miniature, or Petting, Zoo (11), an Upper Zoo (9) more or less surrounding the Children's Zoo and quite a large number of paddock-style exhibits — bison, wolves, beaver and others — in the area around the Miniature Railway (10).

Park Zoos Past and Present
The original zoo was an almost accidental cluster of ad hoc collections along the hillside at the Georgia Street entrance to the park, beginning with an unfortunate black bear tied to a stump by a short length of rope.

Adopted by the first Park Ranger, Henry Avison, and his family, this unorthodox pet lived near their home without incident until one day in 1893 it struck a resounding blow for animal rights. Henry Avison, Jr., recounted the story of that brief rebellion:

"One sunny afternoon, the wife of the Methodist clergyman approached the bear ... and poked it in the ribs with the point of her umbrella. The bear took umbrage and took a swift swipe at its molester.

"The bear's claws caught in the lady's skirt and, in the twinkling of an eye, there was more than her slip showing."

The outcry over respectable women being attacked by wild

animals in a public park prompted the Parks Commissioners, according to Avison, to build what would be the first official permanent zoo structure — a pit. It joined several cages that dated back to 1889.

Arguments over the advisability and morality of a zoo were extant from the beginning. One of the earliest recorded condemnations, however, is contained in a letter from a concerned taxpayer who wrote to the Parks Board in 1904 asking "...what could be done to remedy the evil."

By 1906 the bear pit was viewed as a cruel form of housing for the growing number of ursine incumbents, so cages were erected as a substitute just behind where Lord Stanley's statue (5) stands today. The debate over zoo acquisitions aside, the park quickly became a repository for all manner of species the Parks Board either pursued or reluctantly accepted as hand-me-down gifts from the city. The descendants of some can still be found in Stanley Park.

The precursors of Lost Lagoon's black swans, for instance, were acquired from the New South Wales Zoological Society in 1901; the Park's grey squirrel population can trace its roots to several pairs transferred from the New York Park Department in 1909.

In 1912, following the advice of English landscape designer Thomas Mawson, clearing began for the nucleus of the "modern" Lower Zoo. The only previous modifications had been the construction of a series of pools called the Duck Ponds, a small portion of which still remains today.

While the present zoo prides itself on successfully rearing endangered species and a hands-off attitude towards the Park's indigenous fauna, the approaches of the Parks Board and zoo staff during the first few decades of the 20th century were experimental at best. In an attempt to reduce display birds' predation by raptors, officials set out in 1916 to eradicate hawks and owls. Predictably, the rat population boomed. Faced with the imminent loss of all exotic fowl eggs and nestlings to the furry marauders, the Parks Board rescinded its execution order.

Far more successful was their attempt in 1920 to deal with the problem of boisterous and aggressive mallard flocks. The Board simply shipped off as many as it could catch to the Children's Aid Society — for Christmas dinners.

By 1931 the "new" zoo was already deteriorating and under heavy attack by the Society for the Prevention of Cruelty to Animals. Park authorities subsequently hired an American consultant from Philadelphia to study the existing site and alternatives.

The "expert's" advice? Abandon the current zoo and move the collections to Beaver Lake — with a few hippos and giraffes to add a touch of novelty. The image of hippopotami wallowing in Beaver Lake while puzzled giraffes nibbled fruitlessly on native firs and cedars was, apparently, a more expansive vision than the Parks Board had expected. It ignored the report.

The zoo issue continued to haunt the Park for years. One of the more original proposals came from a newspaper editorial writer who opined in 1947 that a "taxidermy zoo" was the solution. Stuffed animals would take up less room, eat nothing and require little but the odd dusting.

The Lower Zoo Today (7)

Situated south of the Vancouver Public Aquarium, this is the most popular attraction in the entire park, accounting for an estimated 1.2 to 1.5 million visits a year.

Its popularity is a bit difficult to explain considering that the exhibits are few and outdated. In addition, it is definitely not a modern facility. The Monkey House dates to 1950, the Otter Pool to 1952, the Penguin Pool to 1953. The small-animal house was constructed in 1955 and the bear grottoes in 1961.

The lack of anything but modest renovations is easier to identify than the zoo's immense appeal to residents and tourists alike: controversy.

Zoos aren't much in favor by some people, yet are passionately espoused by others. Plans have been suggested for major changes to the existing collections and features. But so far no consensus has been reached as to whether the former should be indigenous species only or a mixture of native ones and the existing exotics. Then, of course, there are those who say that the only good zoo is no zoo.

If a zoo were to be accepted then the issues of siting, preservation of park "natural" spaces and cost, estimated at many millions of dollars, become contentious variables. Then there is the impact a revamped facility would have on traffic and parking. Many are convinced that Stanley Park is already over used. There is scant likelihood that any elected Parks official who advocated pavement as a platform plank would emerge unscathed at the polls.

Still, it's possible that the final disposition of the zoo could be decided in the next year or so. In the meantime, the Lower Zoo is open year-round from 10:00 a.m. daily and is free, one of only three no-charge zoo facilities in Canada. It is also the birthplace of a drama which could be called "The Night of the Penquins" since its most popular residents were the star attractions.

Former zoo manager, Larry LeSage, told the author this story of "fowl" play and madcap marine antics:

LeSage had just managed to get to bed after a particularly long and demanding evening when the telephone rang. It was 2:00 a.m. More than a bit groggy at the rude awakening, LeSage answered. A voice informed him that "his" penguins were cavorting in the ornamental pool in front of City Hall — right across town.

LeSage thanked the caller and hung up. Assuming it was a prank played by a recent house guest, he went back to sleep. But not for long.

The phone rang again. This time the caller identified himself as a police officer. He insisted there really were penguins in the City Hall pool.

LeSage dragged a coat over his pajamas, climbed into his car and set off at high speed for the municipal building.

Not surprisingly, he was stopped. The Constable demanded to know where he was going in such a hurry. Larry told him he had to get his penguins out of the pool at City Hall. The Officer went back to his squad car to check LeSage's story but, suspecting Le-Sage's sobriety or sanity, took the keys with him.

Informed that LeSage was telling the truth, the intrigued Officer not only sent him on his way without a traffic ticket but provided an escort.

By the time they arrived, the pool was the center of a large and boisterous crowd drawn by the flashing lights of other police cruisers. Sure enough, at the center of this noisy nocturnal gathering, were two penguins energetically swimming laps around the civic pool.

LeSage and several policemen attempted to snare the waterfowl from the pool's edge without luck. So he and two of the Officers rolled up their trousers and waded in.

But the bystanders were on the side of the penguins. Every time the pursuers were on the verge of capturing their quarry, the spectators roared encouragement at the birds. Startled by the loud sound, they spurted away from the hunters' clutching hands. Again and again LeSage and his assistants were foiled by the raucous avian boosters.

Finally, the exhausted penguins were cornered by three soaking-wet "co-performers" in the impromptu City Hall circus act and carted back home to their official residence in the park.

The question remains — how did they get there?

Vancouver Public Aquarium (8)

At the north end of the Lower Zoo is a modern complex that attracts over 800,000 paying customers annually: the Vancouver Public Aquarium. It has been a prominent and popular feature of the park since its beginnings as a far more modest facility in June 1956. It now houses the largest number of specimens of any aquarium in North America — 8,900 representing 250 species.

The Aquarium's more memorable exhibits aren't necessarily the Orcas (killer whales), Beluga whales or other large mammals, but the many smaller ones. Hundreds of salt- and fresh-water tanks are colorful homes to spectacular varieties of marine life, many found in no other aquarium on the continent. In addition, there are unusual attractions such as the Graham Amazon Gallery which recreates Amazonian ecosystems, the MacMillan Tropical Gallery (sharks and swordfish a specialty) and several others, such as the B.C. Hall of Fishes and the Rufe Gibbs Hall, which are every bit as fascinating.

But the Aquarium doesn't exist solely for entertainment. It also plays a vital role in the rescue of marine life and marine research, hosts school seminars and tours such as the "Ed-Venture" series which drew over 73,000 students from primary and secondary grades in 1991. In addition, it also is an information-education source for the general public.

Yet the Aquarium, like the Zoo, has its critics.

Although supported by some 40,000 dues-paying members, donations and grants of various kinds, as well as admission fees, and staffed largely by volunteers, the aquarium is seen as detrimental by some. They feel that it is taking advantage of its ever-increasing popularity by continually demanding more and more park space.

The latter statement is true, as is the charge that the Aquarium has reneged on promises made each time that the latest growth spurt would be its last. But it's difficult to condemn a facility which genuinely benefits the scientific and general communities, provides living laboratories for marine research and preservation, enjoys a worldwide reputation for excellence and enhances local tourism.

For time and fee schedules for the Aquarium call 682-1118.

Upper Zoo (9)
This section lies west of the main Zoo and Aquarium. Several trails lead here but the easiest to locate is one leading uphill from the Japanese Memorial. The latter is a tall, tapering column built in 1919 to commemorate Canadians of Japanese descent who died in World War One.

This pathway leads not only to the Upper Zoo but also to the Children's Zoo (11) and the Miniature Railway (10).

Distinguishing them may be confusing for the first-time visitor since they're all more or less incorporated. Basically, the Upper Zoo exhibits are located west of the large Children's Zoo building, and both along and west of the Miniature Railway right-of-way. A practical rule of thumb is that if you don't have to pay to get in, it's the Upper Zoo.

Exhibits displayed for the most part in open paddocks include bison, Arctic wolves, mountain goats and sheep, beaver, kangaroos and deer. Staid though the Upper Zoo may seem, its docile-appearing residents have a few stories that belie this impression.

Stanley Park still retains some of the wilderness in the above 1898 photo. The dense undergrowth typical of a West Coast forest is still an essential feature of the

park, although the heavy moss on the top branches is
no longer so common. The tree in the center is over 11 m
(38 feet) in diameter, overwhelming the man to its left.

Wolves On The Loose

The Arctic wolves may look tame but zoo staff are cautious when they enter their spacious pen. These are still wild animals with an ingrained hunting instinct. Any illusions about the relative positions of wolf and human in the food chain quickly disappear when you're shut inside with the restlessly-padding hunters. I discovered this relationship during a special visit arranged by Zoo Curator Mike MacIntosh.

The 14-year-old daughter of family friends was contemplating a career in veterinary medicine. I asked Mike if it would be possible to show her what was involved in the zoo's behind-the-scenes work. He agreed. We subsequently spent a pleasant hour feeding polar bears, handling snakes, "herding" flamingoes and generally learning something of the daily routine in maintaining the zoo.

Then Mike brought up the subject of wolves.

He thought that Julie and I would benefit from firsthand experience with North America's most efficient carnivores. Would we like to go into the wolf pen with him? Scratch a curator and find a comedian, I thought. But he was serious.

I had the usual qualms. Would Julie be safe? Was this really the kind of thing a responsible adult would do with a young charge? What would her parents think? Was I going to die? But Julie was excited by the offer and Mike calmly reassuring. I said yes.

We slipped in quietly and stood motionless near the gate. Mike suggested we put our hands in our pockets and keep them there. I didn't ask why. The reason was obvious.

Initially, individual wolves flitted nervously to and fro, staying in the far corners, hugging the fences. Occasionally they disappeared behind trees and brush. Whenever they reappeared their heads were invariably turned toward us interlopers.

The change in behavior came with startling rapidity.

Suddenly, they were no longer aimless white ghosts glimpsed at a distance. They had been transformed into a coordinated pack, trotting counter-clockwise in single file, their route an ellipse — with us at its center. Their passage was noiseless. The sounds of panting or muffled footfalls on the hard earth and scrub grass I expected and strained to hear never came. The silence was eerie, almost palpable.

With each revolution the circle shrank; with each lap the wolves' pace increased. All the while their yellow eyes were fixed firmly upon us.

As the gap steadily dwindled my senses heightened to a degree I had experienced only rarely before. Clarity of focus was so acute that each time the wolves moved behind us the sensation was almost painful. The hairs on the nape of my neck stood up. My shoulder muscles tensed.

Still the oval shrank and the wolves drew closer, ever closer.

Then, after a passage that brought the pack to within a few feet of where we were rooted, Mike murmured: "Okay, it's time to get out. Back up quickly and quietly."

Only when I heard the snick of metal on metal as the latch caught after our exit did I realize that, at some point in the past few seconds, I had stopped breathing. I inhaled and exhaled deeply. And broke into a wide grin. So did Julie.

After our encounter I wondered what would happen should the wolves escape. Then I learned that they already had.

Several years previous, before security was tightened at the Upper Zoo, a prankster or misguided philanthropist paid a late night visit to the wolf pen. With a pair of wire-cutters he opened a small hole in the chain-link fence and left.

Only two of the wolves availed themselves of the escape route. But over the next few nights before they were captured fingernails became somewhat shorter on the Zoo staff's tensed fingers. It seems there were reports trickling in of "friendly white Husky dogs running along beside joggers on the Seawall."

In the belief that "what they don't know won't hurt them," no one ever pointed out their error.

The wolves aren't alone in their escapades. Zoo staff still chuckle over the day the chubby, waddling inhabitants of the Beaver Pond made their break for freedom.

When the beaver habitat was under construction, Zoo personnel expressed doubts about the wisdom of lining the bottom of the pond with steel mesh. The builder assured them that it was so sturdy the industrious beaver couldn't possibly chew through it.

The first sign of a problem came when one of the Park's service trucks plunged through the road west of the Beaver Pond.

An investigation revealed that not only had the beaver sliced through the liner but also had dug a tunnel under the road to a wooded area on the far side. There they would emerge, chop down trees with their sharp incisors and drag their plunder back through the tunnel to home.

The mesh was patched, the holes and tunnel filled and the road repaired. The maintenance workers left, satisfied that their job was done. Then the Miniature Railway tracks on the far side of the Beaver Pond began to sag.

Their breakout bid thwarted in one direction, the beaver had simply turned around and begun digging again. This time they had undermined the railway bed.

Which is why, should visitors wonder, the otherwise natural environment of the Beaver Pond site is marred by a concrete-lined pool.

Children's Zoo (11)

The Children's, or Petting, Zoo caused a world-wide sensation when it opened in 1950. The idea of a Zoo where youngsters could have a hands-on, eye-level encounter with various domestic birds and animals was novel enough that Warner Brothers sent a camera crew and featured it in a news reel.

The Children's Zoo is just as popular today — over 40 years later — as it was then and not just with younger family members. The reactions of tykes and toddlers to goats, llamas, cows, sheep, hens and other miniature animal species makes the small admission fee a bargain.

The Children's Zoo is open year-round but may be restricted to weekend admissions during the winter.

Miniature Railway (10)

Would adults even be interested in riding on a miniature train? Oh, yes. Of the more than 700,000 tickets sold each year, well over half are adult fares.

The first Miniature Railway, a timid effort because of fears that it wouldn't attract much interest, went into service in 1947 on the present site of the Children's Zoo. The opportunity for an expanded Miniature Railway resulted from typhoon Frieda that battered British Columbia in 1962. Frieda uprooted or smashed some 3,000 trees in Stanley Park alone, killing one woman and tearing open a substantial clearing. Rather than replant this area, the new Miniature Railway was built.

The engines that pull the small cars are scale replicas of actual locomotives. Two are Chances and one is modelled on the CPR engine #374 which on May 23, 1887, pulled the first train into Vancouver over the new Canadian Pacific Railway. The replica, built by George D. Shannon at the Neilson Machine Works in 1966, attracts legions of admiring shutterbugs.

While the ride only lasts 8-10 minutes and covers just 1 km (roughly 2/3 of a mile) with loop-backs, this is not a "toy" railway. All of the regulations which apply to full-sized Canadian trains apply to the Stanley Park operation. Whistles and signals used are authentic and the Miniature Railway is automatically sent the same updates on railway practices as its big brothers and sisters.

At Christmas, thousands of Vancouverites, especially senior citizens, flock to the Miniature Railway when the track areas are festooned with bright lights and floodlit seasonal tableaux.

The Petting Zoo and the Miniature Railway are both popular — and not just with children. Over half of the Railway's 700,000 passengers a year are adults.

Sidetrip Options
The Checker Board (12) is a hundred meters or so (just over 100 yards) from the Upper Zoo. It was once a much-frequented game.

The gloomy location and battered playing pieces of the Checker Board provide no clues as to why this pastime was such a rage in the 1920s. But in 1922, when this was one of the first outdoor boards built for the Vancouver Checker Association, players and spectators packed the area. Eventually their ardor cooled, the surrounding conifers grew and the roadside attraction was plunged into chilly shade and obscurity.

Stanley Park Pavilion (13)
This Pavilion was part of a large-scale construction program that saw the erection of an enormous bandstand in 1911 and the Pavilion itself in 1913. The area was thereafter for many years the social hub of the Park and much of Vancouver.

With the rustic lodge nestled in the trees as a backdrop, hundreds and sometimes thousands of Vancouverites gathered around the bandstand on the open lawns in front of the Pavilion. Here they listened to the uniformed Parks Board Band play martial and religious airs, the only music permitted by strait-laced Parks officials.

The scene today isn't all that different from nearly a century ago since the exterior of the Pavilion has changed little except for the addition of a west wing in 1923. Of course the Pavilion isn't, with apologies to the current restaurant licensee, the elegant dining and dancing place it used to be. The food concession now is basically cafeteria service.

The Pavilion, however, remains a sentimental favorite with many city residents and visitors who remember the heritage building and facilities in its heyday. They still come for a cup of tea or coffee and enjoy the splendid views from the verandah or dining room of the manicured gardens.

Of the latter, there's one near the Pavilion that few residents or visitors know exists. The Garden of Remembrance (14) is tucked into the shrubbery behind the Pavilion. It's not very large but, as with most small gardens, seems to exist for the viewer's personal pleasure. The wishing well, rockery and pool were built in 1948 by the Women's Auxilliary to the Air Services as a memorial to British and Commonwealth airmen killed in the Second World War.

At the Pavilion are telephones, public washrooms, and limited parking. However, the Upper Zoo parking lot immediately north of the Pavilion is less than a minute's walk away.

Malkin Bowl (15)
Opposite the Pavilion, on the far side of the facing gardens and grassy area, is Malkin Bowl, one of only two open-air theatre and

The bouncy, white-striped animals in Stanley Park, top, are not cats but skunks, very peaceful if left alone. Other free running animals include coyotes, left, and deer, center left. Among birds, the inquisitive Stellars jay, above, is one of the year-round residents. It is also B.C.'s official bird emblem.

music venues in Vancouver. The original bandstand was built in 1911 and replaced in 1934 with the present shell-style one. The cost was borne by Vancouver businessman W. H. Malkin and named the Marion Malkin Bowl in his wife's honor.

Following a series of fires, the Malkin Bowl was restored in 1984 and gives audiences an opportunity to attend Theatre Under The Stars (TUTS) performances in a beautiful outdoor setting. Tickets for TUTS can be obtained from most major ticket sales outlets in Vancouver.

Harding Memorial (16)

On the east side of the open area in front of the Pavilion is an imposing monument flanked by gleaming bronze eagles. Designed by Charles Marega, architect of the Promenade, the Harding Memorial commemorates the visit of Warren G. Harding, who in 1923 became the first American President to set foot on Canadian soil.

One of the most beautiful features of the Harding Memorial can't be seen from the front so few people know it's there. At the rear of the monument is an ornately carved lion's-head fountain set into the wall. Here, also, is a neglected garden that seems to have lain forgotten for many years. Overgrown plaques of various kinds lie under the moss and dead leaves which have accumulated over the decades.

Heron Rookeries

A keen eye is required to identify the rookeries once nesting season is over, but during spring and early summer the constant arrivals and departures of adult great blue herons make their location evident. There are at least eight of these vertical condominiums in the Park, two directly east of the Harding Memorial.

The main Park rookery was destroyed in 1927 when the massive, 166-year-old "Heron Tree" at Brockton Point was removed. At the time it was the nesting site for 27 adult pairs which reared at least 80 young each year. It was feared that these magnificent wading birds would abandon the Park, but smaller rookeries were soon dotted around the area.

Herons are considered "primitive" birds by ornithologists. With their 2.13-m (7-foot) wingspans, slow flapping flight and nerve-grating squawk, they do seem like creatures from another age. Yet a great blue heron, wading with delicate, measured steps, head poised on slender neck as it searches for prey, appears graceful. Silhouetted against an evening sky, erect and motionless at the water's edge, it is a poignant embodiment of the beauty in solitude.

Rose Gardens (17)

Slightly southwest of the Pavilion is the hillside floral display called the Rose Gardens, colorful, fragrant and popular.

How many bushes are there? Even the dedicated Park garden-ers have no idea. They fill one carefully tilled bed after another, spilling across the grassy slopes in a dazzling display of colors from brassy reds to pale creams and buttery yellows. They line pathways, carpet trellises, and cascade in multi-hued fountains.

The names of these exotic hybrids are as much a treat for the tongue as their inspirations are a gift to the eye and nose: Mas-querade, Dame-de-Coeurs, Garden Party and many more.

Begun in 1920 by the Kiwanis community service organization, the goal of the Rose Gardens originators was "to demonstrate the possibilities of Rose Culture in Vancouver." Despite the ravages of mildew, black spot, slugs, aphids, black fly and intemperate rain-fall, their success is evident. The Rose Gardens are open to the public without restriction or charge.

Another floral display is west of the Pipeline Road. Here are some truly magnificent beds containing several hundred species of artfully arranged flowering plants that rival their rose cousins. Dis-plays change with the seasons so each visit offers something excit-ing and new.

Rose Garden Cottage and Service Yard (18)
Below, and at the far northern end of the various flower gardens which fill this area, are two features which may pique visitors' cu-riosity.

The small log building which looks every bit a country cottage is the offices of the Stanley Park Zoological Society. Members of the Society are involved with all facets of the Park and play an im-portant role in guiding and interpretive programs. Anyone inter-ested in this non-profit organization or the special events it sponsors is invited to call 688-2055. Memberships are available to adults and children, with fees embarrassingly modest.

The rambling complex of mismatched buildings behind the cot-tage is the Service Yard. In addition to containing facilities for park work crews it also houses the stables for the Vancouver Police mounted unit and AAA Horse & Carriage, the company which provides the popular horse-drawn carriage tours of Stanley Park, and the Zoo's animal hospital and quarantine area.

The Service Yard may change radically over the next few years. No firm plans have been made but one of the projects which has excited interest is the possibility of an informative and educational interpretive center.

Shakespeare Memorial and Garden (19)
This rather odd monument — well, odd for Stanley Park — is tucked back into a hedge that runs along the side of the southern-most of the Service Yard buildings. (If you'd like an equally odd

reference point, it is almost directly west of the Rose Garden Cottage Moose.)

The Shakespeare Society's intention when it laid out the gardens in the 1930s was to create an area that featured plants and trees of Elizabethan England. Unfortunately, enthusiasm for the project waned after the official opening in 1936. While English trees appropriate to the theme still thrive, efforts at floral tributes long ago withered and died. But here and there are commemorative plaques at the bases of various transplanted trees in the immediate vicinity of the Shakespeare Garden.

The only feature left that is easy to locate is the Memorial itself. Its main column is an unusual combination of brick and stone with a profile of the Bard in relief. The 3-m (nearly 10-foot) memorial is capped with an open half-circle of stone on each of its four sides, with spikes which make the whole seem vaguely crown-like. Unfortunately, those who prefer destroying art rather than creating it have left him with a rather scarred image.

The Playground (20)
In the 1920s the small playground just above the Rose Gardens was the site of one of the first of several outdoor checkerboards

The Vancouver Automobile Club in Stanley Park in 1909. All vehicles are Oldsmobiles except for a single cylinder Packard. The road is surfaced with material from the giant midden described on page 50, the shells resulting in the white color.

but the playground itself is an enigma. No specific mention is made in the Parks Board records as to when it was constructed.

There is, however, an 1896 reference to the B.C. Consolidated Railway and Light Company's purchase of playground equipment for a children's play area. This purchase could have been the fore-runner of the modest swings, slides and other pieces here today. It would have been a logical place for it since here once stood the old zoo's bear cages and a concession stand. From the late 1880s to the early 1900s this area was one of the busiest in the Park.

Primitive cages housed a large menagerie of wild animals which drew crowds and made the small concession stand nearby the most lucrative operated by the Parks Board. In addition, the hillside was a favorite with picnickers, despite the tree stumps which dotted it for several years. The only hint that this was any-thing but a limited playground is that some of the pines appear to grow in straight rows where they formed a line at the back of the cages in the former zoo.

Park Ranger (21)
Between the Playground and the Promenade is the last stop on the Entertainment Loop, although there is nothing to mark it.

Park Ranger Henry Avison and his cottage in 1898. Like the roadway in the photo on pages 88-89, the paths are surfaced with shells excavated from the Indian midden.

The bandstand, below, was a popular Park attraction. It was demolished in the early 1920s and replaced with the present Malkin Bowl.

On top of this slope leading towards the north end of the Promenade once sat the first park structure in the city — the home of Park Ranger Henry Avison.

When he was hired in 1888, his duties were defined as "walking around the Park," putting out fires and preventing timber cutting. During the next 10 years he did that and more, including cutting or clearing trails and inadvertently starting Stanley Park's zoo collection.

The Parks Committee built a home for Avison and his family, belatedly adding a stable and an outhouse. Then the Committee stated that "No other building would be erected in Stanley Park so as to preserve the natural beauty." Ironically, the next three decades witnessed one of the most intense periods of construction in the Park's history.

Avison left his position as Park Ranger in 1898, lured to Alaska along with many thousands of other hopefuls by the Klondike gold rush. In 1947, because of the dedicated efforts of his son, Henry, the path which meanders up the western side of the hairpin turn approaching Prospect Point became officially known as the Avison Trail.

End of Walk II
Because Walk II is a loop, you're now back at the Promenade. From here are two short side trips.

The first is an easy one: cross back over the Promenade and take a short walk along the Seawall. You can go left and follow the north shore of Coal Harbour or right and cross into Devonian Harbour Park to look at the expensive yachts.

The second is to descend the slope to the right of the Promenade, heading off on an oblique angle towards Lost Lagoon. You'll notice an arch that allows you to pass underneath Georgia Street. Lost Lagoon is just on the other side. You can make this a brief visit or enjoy parts or all of Walk IV which describes this popular artificial lake and its perimeter trail.

An alternative way to arrive at Lost Lagoon is by walking back across the Promenade. The broad path at the far end dips down under the Causeway and emerges at Lost Lagoon. This latter route is wheelchair accessible.

Canada geese are familiar, year-round residents. Although people enjoy feeding the geese and other waterfowl, they unfortunately often do more harm than good. Parks officials stress that popcorn, bread, and other food unnatural to the birds is injurious. Substitute wild bird feed which is available at many stores.

STANLEY PARK WALKS: III

BEAVER LAKE — DISTANCE: 2.3 KM (1.4 MILES)
The Beaver Lake Walk is not confined to a simple circuit of this water body. It is a linear itinerary, not a loop, that begins on the south shore of Lost Lagoon, briefly follows its eastern edge then heads into the forest to Beaver Lake. From there it descends Beaver Lake Creek to its mouth on the Narrows or Burrard Inlet, the north side of the park.

(Directions at the end of this walk bring the visitor back to the Lost Lagoon starting point by following one of several optional routes. The shortest entails a walking time of roughly 30 minutes; the longest, approximately two hours. To Beaver Lake Creek exit takes 45 minutes to an hour.)

What Will You See?
The major advantage of this walk is that it unfurls a great deal of Stanley Park's attributes.

You can start by feeding the ducks, geese, swans and anything else that swims, flies, waddles or walks at Lost Lagoon. An important point to remember, however, is that the cute, cat-sized creatures with black and white stripes and rolling gait are skunks.

Many visitors, judging by their reckless behavior around these furry animals, aren't familiar with their chief method of defence. If

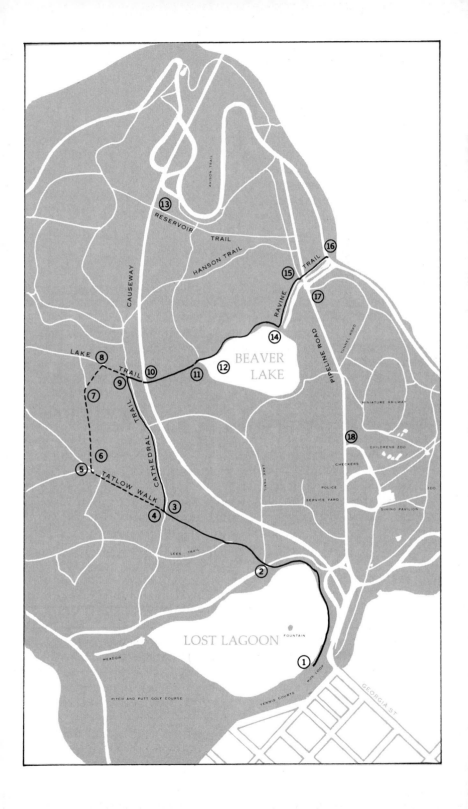

alarmed, adults and young alike can spray a perceived threat with a choking, eye-stinging substance that stinks far worse than anything you may have encountered. It is very difficult to neutralize or wash off, with tomato juice the folk remedy that seems most effective. The best advice is to observe them from a distance and stay out of their way.

You'll also have a chance to plunge into the forested heart of the park with its legions of squirrels, perhaps a coyote or two, lily-pad covered Beaver Lake and a short stretch of creek where salmon and trout spawn.

On the far side are great views of Burrard Inlet, the Coast Mountains and perhaps seals bobbing in the kelp beds close to the shore. Depending on the return option, you can enjoy the Seawall, Zoos, Aquarium, Rose Gardens and much more.

The Starting Point
The Beaver Lake Walk begins at the southeast corner of Lost Lagoon (1) on the west side of Georgia Street. Follow the lakeside path, walking counterclockwise around the end of Lost Lagoon. Roughly 100 m (110 yards) after the path begins to curve back towards the west, a dirt path leads up the grassy slope. Turn off here.

The trail immediately crosses a narrow paved road. On the other side of the road is a signposted fork (2). Take the left path, the one called Tatlow Walk, which indicates the way to Ferguson Point and Third Beach, but don't be confused. We're not going to either.

Note: closely follow the upcoming sets of directions. Because signposting in the forest is spotty, trail descriptions between here and Beaver Lake are critical.

Within the first 50 m (55 yards) in the large tree stumps are good examples of what loggers called "springboard holes." They are two or more very deep holes at or slightly above head level. Because the base of a large tree was quite wide and had no commercial value, fallers (the proper name for someone who "drops" a tree) cut these deep notches and inserted the narrow tongue of a wide plank into each to create a platform. With such platforms on opposing sides, two fallers standing on them were able to each take an end of the enormous cross-cut saw they wielded.

In some cases, especially with massive cedars, the trees were so broad at the bottom, or butt end, that fallers needed to notch a second set of springboard holes above the first to clear the spreading base. In others, it was necessary to steadily work right around a tree to cut through it, accounting for the "ring" of springboard holes on some stumps.

The area on each side of the path is typical of coastal forest.

It's damp, mossy and broken here and there by dark pools of stagnant water. The bushes with the leathery and shiny broad leaves are salal. Small, bell-like, downward-pointing rows of pink flowers on these shrubs develop purple berries, once a common Native food. The fruit was pressed into cakes, dried, and eaten when other fresh provender was scarce during winter months. Today, salal is a staple of floral arrangements, prized for its firm, glossy foliage.

The boggy conditions here are also ideal for another plant, the skunk cabbage, often smelled before it is seen. It gives off a musky scent, especially in spring and early summer, and its wide leaves and bright yellow inner part adding an exotic and colorful touch to the boggy forest floor.

Now comes yet another fork — keep to the right. Some 200 m (about 220 yards) from this fork is an intersection that was one of Stanley Park's most popular sites.

Seven Sisters (3)
Known collectively as the Seven Sisters, the fir and cedar trees which stood here were almost a park trademark. In fact, Tatlow Walk was cut in 1911 solely to provide visitors with access to the awe-inspiring grove of forest giants. Today, only the remnants of their decaying stumps remain. In 1951 because of the severe risk posed by the ancient and dying spires, all were with great reluctance cut down.

CHOICES, CHOICES
The Seven Sisters intersection is marked by a small plaque. This Walk continues by taking the right-hand path, although there is a slight optional diversion which might be of interest. If you choose the former, skip this next section and continue to the next intersection along Cathedral Trail where Lake Trail (9) meets it.

If you're curious about the optional diversion, instead of bearing right, go straight ahead along Tatlow Walk (4).

There are some massive Western Red Cedars along the way, including several which are "untopped."

Roughly 60 years ago the Parks Board decided that the dead upper portions, or "spikes," of these cedars would be less dangerous and the forest canopy more pleasing to the eye if they were lopped off, or "topped."

The cedar was of incredible importance to the Native Peoples of the Coast since their way of life was intimately bound up with this magnificent tree. It provided material for shelter, clothing, eating utensils, thread, canoe-building, totem carving and more. Several legends which explain how cedar came to be were passed from generation to generation in the Pacific Northwest. The following is such a story:

"Long ago, when the world was newly formed, the Great Spirit

Opposite page: Oxen hauling logs over a skid road in 1885 and, above, an old skid road in Stanley Park in 1896. Many of today's trails in the Park were originally built for skidding logs.

created a tribe of giants to dwell on the land beside the sea. All lived in harmony in that far-off time; all creatures could communicate with each other and there was no sickness or death.

"But then the giants began to quarrel and the sound of their bickering disturbed the Great Spirit. To put an end to the noise he decided to turn the giants into trees and create a new race of little people in their stead. But one family of the giants hadn't fought as the others had; what, the Great Spirit asked, could he do for them?

"The good family of giants thought about this for some time and then replied that they would like to become trees like their disgraced kin, but that they wished to be made cedars so that they could forever share the gifts of the Great Spirit with the tribes of little people.

"Happy with their decision, the Great Spirit granted them their wish and that is how cedar came to the land."

At the next major intersection on the Tatlow Walk optional route, there are the remains of a fallen Western Red Cedar (5).

It originally stood 58.8 m (193 feet) tall and was an estimated 720-780 years old. Assuming the latter would mean that it was a seedling around the time that tea was still a novelty in Japan, Liverpool and Amsterdam had just been founded, and the Crusades were a major topic of the day.

To join up with the original Beaver Lake Walk, take the right-hand path (6) and follow it to the next junction (7). Also turn right at the next intersection (8) and you'll be on the Lake Trail. Just ahead is the junction (9) of the Lake and Cathedral Trails — don't turn off, go straight ahead.

For those who didn't take the option, turn right onto the Lake Trail. In a minute or so you'll hear the roar of traffic and come to a green metal pedestrian and equestrian span (10) over the Bridge Highway.

On the far side, the trail is paved for a few meters (yards) before returning to gravel. Shortly after this change of surfacing material is another one of those darned trail forks. Ignore the left-hand path marked Ravine Creek Trail, keep going straight and suddenly you're walking along the north side of Beaver Lake.

Beaver Lake (12)
To the Native People it was "Ahka-Chu" — the "little lake." The name was not only apt but also is becoming more appropriate each year because Beaver Lake is shrinking.

I think you'll agree that it's a beautiful sight. Wood duck families pushing through the water weeds, great blue herons stalking keen-eyed along the shore, lily-pads in bloom — pink- yellow- and white-flowering varieties turn Beaver Lake into an Impressionist's canvas in August — while all around this sunny littoral are towering trees, with fruit-heavy bushes adding color and variety.

But Beaver Lake is very nearly gone. In 1911 its deepest section only measured 1.2 m (4 feet); in 1938 the depth was the same but the area had decreased. Despite removal of dead trees and other debris in 1918 and dredging in 1929, open water was hard to find. By 1985, surveys revealed that lake size had fallen to 4.28 ha (10.58 acres).

The decline of such water bodies is usually a natural event. As dead vegetation rots, it consumes oxygen; the more material there is to decompose, the more oxygen it takes. But when oxygen demand exceeds supply, unrotted vegetation begins to accumulate and the lake gets shallower. This process also decreases the amount of water there is to hold oxygen and the build-up process accelerates.

Eventually the lake becomes swamp, then wet meadow, then dry meadow and perhaps forest. This transformation is happening in Beaver Lake. Unfortunately, the process has been hastened by meddling.

In 1937, it was decided to add water lilies and other aquatic plants to both Lost Lagoon and Beaver Lake. The program failed at the former and succeeded far too well at the latter. The situation, however, isn't entirely negative. The lily-pads are gorgeous, while brown bullheads, catfish and cutthroat trout manage to survive in the cool water and the dense foliage provides a haven for wild-fowl.

The first person to admire Beaver Lake was Captain Stamp, but not for its beauty. In 1865 the ambitious businessman intended building a large sawmill in the Park and use Beaver Lake as water for his boilers.

At the time on maps it was known simply as "the pond," "lake" or "the old lake," but in 1907 beaver were seen and may have inspired the current name. By 1911, maps and other documents were referring to it as Beaver Lake. That year it also became a major recreation area when the perimeter trail was built and a path cut along Beaver Lake Creek to the Narrows side of the Park. Also installed were a sluice gate at the head of Beaver Lake Creek and several small waterfalls.

In addition, that November the Parks Board made one of its periodic blunders — one that would draw snickers from a future generation of Stanley Park Zoo staff. It tried to establish a beaver preserve at the lake, complete with what they assumed was restrictive metal mesh to protect surrounding trees. It didn't. The plan was scrapped.

Then in 1916, the Board accepted an offer from the Vancouver Angling Society to establish a fish hatchery at Beaver Lake. During the next 30 years hundreds of thousands of salmon and trout were stocked in the lake and at least three different hatchery develop-

Beaver appeared in Stanley Park in 1907. For many years their superb tree cutting and tunnelling skills gave the Parks Board an ongoing headache.

ments operated. The last of these (13) was on the small creek which runs into the northwest end of Beaver Lake and some 500 m (550 yards) south of Prospect Point. It's now a leaf-mulching yard.

The hatchery was abandoned in 1946 for reasons of expense yet, surprisingly, some hardy trout linger in the lake. Too, it was discovered a few years ago that Beaver Lake Creek is once again supporting at least a few breeding salmon after an absence of wild stocks since before World War One.

Beaver Lake Creek (14)

The stream is marked by a rustic handrail near the lake's eastern edge. Paths follow both sides of the creek, with the right-hand one keeping more or less to high ground and the other at water level for much of its 300 m (about 330 yards).

On either, it's only a few minutes walk to Beaver Lake Creek's exit at the Seawall. This short distance, however, doesn't detract from its appeal.

Along the way the trail passes under two bridges. The first (15)

100

is Ravine Bridge, a plank one over which passes the Pipeline Road, so-named for the pipes which once carried the city's water supply through Stanley Park. The second is a stone-faced structure (16) built in 1930.

Through the latter is the Seawall with the forest at your back and a vista that includes green-clad mountains, the dark blue waters of Burrard Inlet and a sweeping panorama of the North Shore.

To return to your starting point there are several choices. The shortest way to Lost Lagoon is to take the right-hand sidewalk along Pipeline Road. You'll arrive where you began in about 30 minutes, passing through the Rose Gardens and eventually under the Causeway to the east end of Lost Lagoon.

The Seawall route is the longest and you can turn either right or left. Right will take you past Lumberman's Arch, Brockton Point Lighthouse, Fishermen's Cove, Deadman's Island and along Coal Harbour to within sight of Lost Lagoon.

The left turn runs under the Lions Gate Bridge, then past Prospect Point, Third Beach, Ferguson Point and Second Beach. From Second Beach you can see Lost Lagoon off to your left.

Both Seawall hikes are about the same length — roughly 4.5 km (2.8 miles) and take an hour or slightly less, depending on your pace and stops along the way.

The route via Lumberman's is a compromise, not as long as the Seawall alternatives and infinitely more interesting than the fast track down Pipeline Road.

Turn right onto the Seawall but follow it only to Lumberman's Arch where the children's water park is. Turn right, going under the archway where there are washrooms. When you emerge on the other side you'll note a concession stand to your right and the Stanley Park Zoo-Vancouver Public Aquarium complex straight ahead. Take the paved path in front of you and you can stroll through the Zoo on your way back to Lost Lagoon.

Plan on a 45-minute walk if you choose this option.

For more information on the Seawall, consult Walk I. The Lumberman's Arch-Zoo Area is described in Walk II.

Second Beach in 1933 when the saltwater pool opened. The Park's two beaches have been popular for over a century.

STANLEY PARK WALKS: IV

SIWASH ROCK - THE BLUFFS

This Walk offers some of the best views in Stanley Park, with the bonus that it is one of the least-trafficked areas. For solitude and a chance to gaze out across English Bay towards Vancouver Island without having to contend with a crowd, this is the Walk.

It also offers an intimate look at the Park's forested interior, hints on where to find abandoned military fortifications, a guided tour of some of the area's most unique trees, and a virtual guarantee of stumbling over rabbits. Lots of rabbits.

Plan on approximately an hour of fairly vigorous walking to cover the 2.45 km (1.5 miles). Although the route isn't long, it entails some uphill and downhill travel. While it is not a circuit as such, several return options are at the end of this section so you won't be stranded in the middle of Stanley Park's unofficial Bunny Zone.

WARNING: The Bluffs portion of this walk is safe if you stay on the path and obey restriction signs. But parents must be aware that young children can easily slip between the rungs of the rustic fencing which marks the cliff edges and drop-offs.

NO ONE, CHILD OR ADULT, SHOULD GO BEYOND FENCES OR ENTER ANY AREA WHERE DANGER SIGNS ARE POSTED.

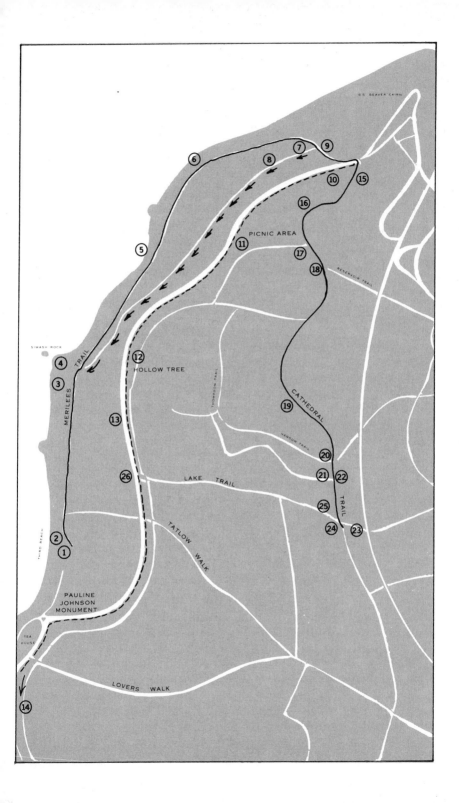

Starting point is Stanley Park's western shore at Third Beach, a beautiful, wave-tossed cove with a curving expanse of clean sand and coastal vistas.

On the water side of the concession stand is a wooden platform (1). Stand with your back to the water and look to your left at the thin screen of trees between the asphalt path and the top of the slope running down to the Seawall. One of those trees (2) is reputedly the largest of its species in North America.

It is a red alder 29.6 m (97 feet) high, with a girth of 5.8 m (nearly 19 feet). This size apparently places it firmly in the arboreal equivalent of the Guinness Book of Records. It also marks the path we're about to take.

The trail is paved for a short distance but becomes gravel as it climbs a gradual hill. It used to be part of the original park perimeter road before it was relocated farther back from the beach. At the top of what is a progressively steeper slope is a fork (3). Bear left, taking time to enjoy the scene framed by a small lookout, before plunging downhill on the Merilees Trail.

Roughly 9 m (30 yards) downhill, look upwards and see if you can locate the weathered timber crossbars nailed a good 21 m (70 feet) off the ground in a very large Douglas fir on the water side of the path. These decaying pieces of wood are all that remain of a World War One observation post. Why anyone would build it becomes apparent very shortly.

Finishing the descent, veer to your left. Although it may not resemble a picnic area now, this is why the area was cleared in 1914. Then World War One broke out, the grounds were sealed off and the heights were converted into an artillery battery.

It seemed a logical choice at the time, although describing an ammunition bunker, a tree-top platform and two 10-cm (4-inch) navy surplus guns as "a naval fortress" was a trifle pretentious. Still, from here and other artillery batteries around English Bay, any approaching enemy vessel would be an easy target.

Fear of an attack was quite real at the time. When Great Britain declared war on Germany, the cruiser *Leipzig* was in San Francisco while four other German cruisers — the *Nurnberg, Scharnhorst, Dresden* and *Gneiseau* — were reported to have left their China stations and were heading into the Pacific. Later reported off Cape Flattery, it was assumed that their destination would be Canadian coastal cities. Near panic ensued.

Engineers immediately began constructing artillery positions at vantage points all around English Bay. Large-calibre guns were stripped from several warships, dragged to the "fortresses" and bolted into place. The waters of English Bay were then divided into "fire zones" and gun crews awaited the appearance of enemy marauders.

None ever came.

Military installations became part of Stanley Park during both World Wars. Below is an artillery and searchlight installation in World War Two at Ferguson Point and, opposite, members of the Canadian Women's Army Corps who were stationed in the Park.

A naval battery on the sandstone bluffs above Siwash Rock in World War One.

By mid-1915 hysteria had abated. Military commanders stripped the fortifications of equipment and personnel. In 1916 the picnic grounds were restored and left in peace until 1938 when a new world conflict seemed inevitable.

This time the former gun battery became a searchlight battery, with a powerful light installed in the odd-shaped bunker which today serves as a convenient lookout point (4). It provides a bird's-eye view of Siwash Rock, English Bay, Kitsilano, Point Grey, the Coast Mountains, West Vancouver and, far to the west, the hazy outline of Vancouver Island.

From the bunker, keep to your immediate left, taking the downward trail (5).

NOTE: A rustic-style pole fence along the water side of this path and frequent warning signs are intended to deter anyone from plunging over the sandstone bluffs to a fairly certain death on the Seawall 18 m (60 feet) below. As already mentioned, resist the temptation to slip between the rails, and ensure that children are strictly supervised in this area.

A sharp upward stretch of trail leads to the highest point of the sandstone bluffs that form an imposing wall along this entire flank of the Park. It is broken only by the ancient lava extrusions which appear as dark grey, fractured rock jutting through the softer sandstone, the same as at Siwash Rock (See Walk I for details on this latter landmark).

This cliff-top vantage point is one of the best places in the Park to see bald eagles. Spring and early summer seem the peak periods for these raptors, with several overhanging Douglas firs along the bluffs the favorite perches for a half-dozen or more at a time. They seem confident they're in no danger and are close enough for ideal photographic opportunities.

From here it's downhill again. Eventually the path swings upwards, and partway there is quite an obvious fork (6). Take the left-hand branch. Here is one final and lovely view of the sea with a log-carved bench to entice visitors to rest for a few moments.

The trail now hooks slightly to the right and meanders upwards away from the water. Several old stumps still showing evidence of springboard holes (described in Walk III) can be seen along the way.

It isn't long before the path reaches the foot of a flight of wooden steps and another trail (7) that provides an option of a shortcut to Third Beach.

If you wish to return to Third Beach rather than continue with the remainder of this walk, turn right onto the trail shown as (7) on your map. It meanders through a largely untouched section of the original Stanley Park forest, running parallel to and slightly below the Park Driveway. Almost immediately after leaving the

These photos from the early 1900s show that the Hollow Tree has long been a favorite with visitors.

wooden stairs, you'll come to a fork — keep to the main path now shown as (8) on the map. At the next branch turn right, back to the Merilees Trail. Then just retrace your steps to Third Beach.

If you press on, climb to the top of the steps and then turn left (9). A few seconds later you'll strike the Park Driveway and another shortcut return option. If you turn right, and stay on the sidewalk (10) down the west side of the road, a few minutes away is Ferguson Point and the cut-off down to Third Beach (1).

On your way is a picnic area (11) on the other side of the road. It sits on top of the former city water reservoir. The concrete flower box near the road with "1904" incised on the outside is a window to history. It is the last surviving water trough to the days when horses, not cars, were the favored mode of park transportation.

The next feature, the Hollow Tree (12), is also on the far side of the Park Driveway, about 500 m (roughly 550 yards) farther.

Actually, it's more of a Hollow Stump these days, but the massive ruin still draws legions of photographers. So popular was the Hollow Tree at one time that the Parks Board licenced concessionaires who ran a thriving photographic business based solely on the novelty of this famous Stanley Park landmark. Although the stump now measures only 17.1 m (56 feet) around, several decades ago its girth was officially recorded as 18.3 m (60 feet).

The surrounding meadow is also the "Bunny Zone" where free-ranging rabbits, descended from discarded pets, hop about by the score. While they're a favorite with photographers and younger family members, just four of these twitching-nosed nibblers can eat as much vegetation in one day as an adult sheep, plus all the junk food they can find.

Still, they have more to worry about than the high-cholesterol snacks from cooing tourists. Owls, hawks, the Park's resident fox and a family of coyotes keep their population in check.

Back on the sidewalk again you have an opportunity to visit another famous Stanley Park giant, the National Geographic Tree (13).

After passing the Hollow Tree, the first dirt path on your right side leads down to a gigantic Western Red Cedar that appeared in *National Geographic* Magazine. To reach it, take the path for a minute or so, looking for it on your left side. It is difficult to miss.

With a circumference of 13.5 m (44 feet, 4 inches), it has attracted attention for well over a century. One of the earliest known photographs of this natural wonder was taken in 1890. Unfortunately, people and nature have taken their toll. It was first topped to its present 39.6 m (130 feet), then a massive branch which protruded from its southwest flank crashed down in a wind storm.

Once you have returned to the roadway, you can stop either at Ferguson Point and Third Beach or keep on the road all the way to Second Beach (14). For this route cross the Park Driveway, and head onto the right fork (15) on the far side. The branch should be marked by a fire hydrant in the middle. (Because so little signposting has been done, it is important that visitors make careful note of trails they encounter from here on. They're critical to this Walk.)

Once on the right fork, the path takes a pronounced curve to the right as it skirts Prospect Point picnic area and the site of the former city reservoir (11), already described on the other return option. Coming out of the curve is another trail to the right but keep left (17). Shortly afterwards there's another branch: go straight ahead (18) and the trail begins to drop downhill. Part of the way down this incline, on the right-hand side, is a very large Western Red Cedar (19) of impressive proportions. A closer inspection reveals that it is not one but two trees joined at the base.

Don't veer at the next intersection (20): keep straight ahead. Almost immediately there will be another path to the right (21) and across from it a fallen colossus of the forest (22), yet another Western Red Cedar.

Just ahead is a main junction where four paths converge to mark the end of Walk IV.

From here you can take any of several optional routes. If you go left (23) you'll soon cross over the Bridge Highway and arrive at Beaver Lake (see Walk III for directions and details). Straight ahead (24) for a few minutes is Lost Lagoon. (This trail is covered in Walk III, Lost Lagoon in Walk V.) The path to the right (25) joins the Park Driveway (26) a few hundred meters (or yards) north of the Ferguson Point Teahouse and Third Beach (1). Both are described in the Seawall tour, Walk I.

NOTE: Until a comprehensive sign system is implemented for trails in the Stanley Park interior, it is quite easy to miss a fork or take the wrong path. Don't be too surprised if it happens to you. Even the author, who is far more familiar with the trails and should know better, finds himself having to retrace his steps with embarrassing regularity. It does, however, add a slight element of adventure to the experience.

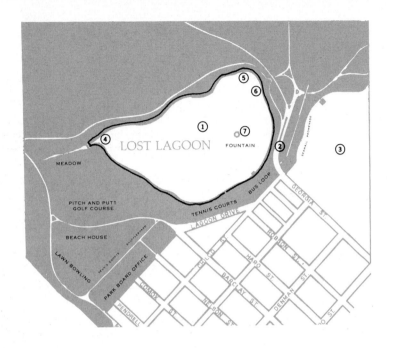

STANLEY PARK WALKS: V

LOST LAGOON

A short walk, 1.75 km (1.1 miles), this area is probably the most popular in Stanley Park for a leisurely stroll. And, unlike some of the interior sections of the park, the lack of signs or other trail markers isn't a problem. Just follow the water's edge to arrive back where you started.

Another difference is that this really isn't a guided tour with a set itinerary as the other walks. Choose a starting point and simply refer to this description and history of the artificial lake when you wish.

Birds, birds, birds. Lost Lagoon is a bird feeder's delight. No coaxing or cajoling is required to draw the hundreds — and sometimes thousands — of ducks, geese and swans.

Although the lake has a resident avian population, its position on the Pacific Flyway also makes it a logical stop for migrating wildfowl. This location accounts for the incredible diversity of species at various times of the year.

Great blue herons hunt the marshy edges, showing a preference for the willow-draped western margin, and three species of swans glide to and fro, graceful at rest, startlingly violent when defending territory. Canada geese waddle along — and foul — the

Entrance to Stanley Park in 1940, with Lost Lagoon on the left. The land between Lost Lagoon and Second Beach has been radically altered. One change is that uncontrolled populations of Canada geese have stripped away the lawns bordering the stream below, resulting in heavy bank erosion.

The Seven Sisters, a spectacular grove of fir and cedar which
had to be removed because of their age. (See page 95.)

paths and grassy surrounding slopes, competing fiercely with flocks of mallard ducks. Occasionally, even bald eagles plunge into the lake's shallow water to seize unwary fish.

The margin of the lake also draws other wildlife. Deer sometimes venture to the northern shore while raccoons seem to favor the west corner. Both areas are also favored by several families of fairly tame, but unpredictable, skunks. Squirrels can be found anywhere in the park, the perimeter of Lost Lagoon no exception. Most are brave, or greedy, enough to eat out of your hand.

Lost Lagoon has also acquired a small amphibian population of several turtles. Since turtles aren't native to the lake, they are, in all probability, emancipated pets. But whether their owner did them a favor remains to be seen.

Saltwater Bay To Freshwater Lake

One aspect of Lost Lagoon that even Vancouver residents don't realize is that it is not a natural lake. What is now a fresh-water body 16.6 ha (just over 41 acres) in area was simply the head of Coal Harbour (3) until 1916 when the Causeway (2) was built.

Prior to then, Lost Lagoon was a muddy basin at low tide and the shallow, salt-water western end of Coal Harbour (3) at high tide. As already mentioned a canoeist could, when conditions were right, paddle to the western end, enter the creek there, follow the stream through to Second Beach and then travel clockwise around the park back to Coal Harbour without having to portage.

Native food gatherers valued the odorous, exposed mud flats as a major source of clams. Indeed, a large Native dwelling once stood on the north side of the basin (5) where clamshell remains indicate a large Indian midden. The Coal Basin a name given to the Lost Lagoon end of the bay to distinguish it from the deeper Coal Harbour portion, also supported several rudimentary pioneer cabins until late in the 1800s.

One of the first items of business when Stanley Park was created in 1888 was to link it to Georgia Street with a bridge. Until late that year, anyone wishing to walk from Georgia Street onto the Government Reserve had to cross a log anchored in the muddy shallows. The Parks Board consequently purchased a bridgehead at the southern end of Coal Basin, building a wooden span soon after. This bridge still allowed tidal waters to flow beneath the heavy timbered frame.

In 1905 it was suggested that the bridge be replaced with a solid embankment or causeway, the basin drained and a grass field built in its stead. The Parks Board endorsed this plan but, lacking funds, put the project on indefinite hold. Although they didn't realize it, the issue of what to do with the future Lost Lagoon became one of the first of many hotly-contested public debates that in forthcoming years would swirl around Stanley Park.

By the end of 1909, the Parks Board had formal plans for a causeway, modified next year to incorporate sluice gates that would permit some flow of water into and out of Coal Basin.

The same year the southern side of Lost Lagoon became part of Stanley Park when the city designated the strip as parkland. All of the houses were moved in 1913, with the exception of one now used as a daycare center.

A causeway was authorized in 1912 and intense public debate over the fate of Lost Lagoon began. The Vancouver Trades and Labour Council, a workers' organization, declared itself adamantly opposed to what it termed an artificial lake. It espoused filling the basin and turning it into a playground.

Every major Union backed this view in what a latter-day researcher described as a class-line dispute. In a subsequent public referendum, white-collar workers voted overwhelmingly for a lake, blue-collar ones for a sports or playing field. The pro-lake forces won.

The next battle would be over the kind of lake.

An English landscape architectural firm, T. Mawson and Associates, who had designed the Zoo, Prospect Point, Brockton Point Lighthouse and the main Park entrance, were hired to design several options. Of four choices, the Parks Board chose one that envisaged construction of an artificial lake with a sports stadium on the northwest side and an ornate museum edifice on the southwest shore. It also approved Mawson's design for an upgraded park road and a formal zoo.

There was an immediate public uproar.

One letter to the editor, hysterically inaccurate but indicative of the furor raging, claimed that "of a total of 960 acres in the park, 210 acres would be denuded of trees."

An editorial condemning City Council's endorsement of the Parks Board project slammed the hiring of an architect uninterested in anything but "classical gardens," adding "They must build in the grand manner. There must be the maximum of artificiality and as little as possible of nature."

The Mawson design was shelved. The deciding factor was money. The stadium alone would have cost $800,000. To put this amount in perspective, skilled tradesmen were making $4.50 for an eight-hour work day, with the average Canadian earning less than $800 a year. The Parks Board's offices rented for $56 a month, and the basic budget for the entire parks and recreation system was $45,000.

Between 1913 and 1916 houses along the future lagoon's southern shore were eliminated and the Parks Board began building a causeway at the foot of Georgia Street by the cheapest means pos-

Lost Lagoon in 1868 when it was part of Coal Harbour. Over the decades architects and Parks Commissioners have had many ideas about how it should be utilized, including the Museum and Art Gallery Complex, below. Fortunately, lack of funds resulted in preservation of most of the Lagoon.

PACIFIC MUSEUM VANCOUVER
PERSPECTIVE VIEW

Canada's famous Metis poet, Pauline Johnson, and her memorial in Stanley Park.

sible. Ashes and city street sweepings were trucked to the site and simply dumped into the gap beneath the bridge.

By 1916 the filling was finished, but not until 1922 would the newly formed lake have its current name, Lost Lagoon. The source of this evocative title was a poem written by Emily Pauline Johnson, Canada's famous Metis poet.

The daughter of a Mohawk chief and an Englishwoman, Johnson was born on the Six Nations Reserve near Brantford, Ontario, in 1861. She gained widespread fame as an "Indian poetess" and acted as a Canadian cultural ambassador during her speaking engagements in the United States and Britain between 1892 and 1910.

She published several books of poetry and Native legends, one of which contained a poem inspired by her experience of Coal Harbour and its muddy western extreme, Coal Basin. She called this brief work *The Lost Lagoon*:

"It is dusk on the Lost Lagoon,
And we two dreaming the dusk away,
Beneath the drift of a twilight grey,
Beneath the drowse of an ending day,
And the curve of a golden moon.

"It is dark in the Lost Lagoon,
And gone are the depths of haunting blue,
The grouping gulls, and the old canoe,
The singing firs, and the dusk and — you,
And gone is the golden moon.

"O! lure of the Lost Lagoon, —
I dream tonight that my paddle blurs
The purple shade where the seaweed stirs,
I hear the call of the singing firs
In the hush of the golden moon."

Despite questions as to whether the subject was Lost Lagoon, Johnson herself left no doubt about her inspiration:

"I have always resented that jarring unattractive name [Coal Harbour] for years. When I first plied paddle across the gunwhale of a light canoe and idled about the margin, I named the sheltered little cove Lost Lagoon. This was just to please my own fancy for, as that perfect summer month drifted on, the ever restless tides left the harbor devoid of any water at my favorite canoeing hour and my pet idling place was lost for many days; hence my fancy to call it Lost Lagoon."

Johnson died in Vancouver in 1913. The Parks Board gave special permission for her to be buried in Stanley Park in accordance with her wishes, selecting a secluded site at Ferguson Point. Following the dedication of a memorial to her in 1922, the Parks Board officially named the lake Lost Lagoon in Johnson's honor.

The next step in Lost Lagoon's transformation came in 1929 when it became a true fresh-water lake. Salt water still entered through pipes from Coal Harbour, but the B.C. Fish and Game Protection Association was given permission to shut these off and that fall begin stocking the lake with trout.

Anglers were charged $1 a rod to help defray costs. As a result, the Parks Board's boat-and-canoe concession became a lucrative enterprise. The stocking experiment also was a success. The Stanley Park Flyfishing Association reported in 1932 that its members were regularly catching cutthroat trout weighing from one-half kilogram (1 pound) to 2 kg (nearly 4.5 pounds).

At no time in its lengthy history has Stanley Park lacked suggestions from the public and even the Parks Board itself for ways to "improve" this popular recreation area. Sometimes the ideas have had merit but the Park has attracted crackpots as often as more sensible types. Lost Lagoon has had its share of both.

For example, the lilies added to the eastern shore (6) in 1930 seem to have been a welcome addition, but other projects proposed and rejected have included a fountain with a concealed phonograph, a miniature train to run around the shoreline, a dance hall and refreshment pavilion, and a power boat raceway.

Others which seemed crazy to many went ahead anyway.

For Vancouver's 50th anniversary in 1936 a $35,000 fountain (7) was built, opposed by many citizens who waged war in the city's newspapers. Some decried the cost in the middle of the Great Depression, while others found it ugly. One writer blasted it as "...gilding nature's lilies for the purpose of fatuous goggling." Another said the expense could not be justified when "people in the city are starving."

Even proponents weren't lavish in their praise. According to one, "By night the fountain is a beautiful sight ... by daylight the squat, moth-coloured structure is an eyesore."

So vitriolic and sustained was the abuse heaped on the Parks Board and its project that, when considering an appropriate gift for the Right Honourable Earl of Derby, son of Stanley Park's dedicator, one Parks Commissioner quipped "Why don't we give him the fountain?"

With the addition in 1938 of the walkway that circumnavigates the lake, "meddling" at Lost Lagoon more or less came to an end. Apart from declaring it a wild bird sanctuary the same year, eliminating boats (young boys were said to be using them to "liberate" ducks and geese by "cracking them over the head with oars") and improving the shoreline with viewing platforms, Lost Lagoon today looks much as it did several decades ago.

The only noticeable changes today are the seasons — each with its own beauty. In spring there are tender greens of new growth, a pink frosting of cherry blossoms to the east and, forming a spectacular background, the cloak of the forest against the distant snow-covered mountains.

In summer the paths, water and grassy margins are a fluffy mass of newly hatched ducklings and goslings, learning the art of panhandling with clumsy enthusiasm to the delight of even the most jaded observer.

In fall the lake takes on a poignant aspect, its dark surface covered with fallen leaves in golds and speckled browns, while Canada geese grow restless and fly sorties back and forth in preparation for the coming exodus to the south.

In winter Lost Lagoon becomes a refuge for migratory transients by the thousands as flocks of ducks of every description arrive to rest for the arduous journeys ahead. On cold mornings, grasses and sedges at the water's edge become brittle stalagmites of glittering crystal, weakly reflecting light which itself seems chilled and subdued, filtered through a somber, gunmetal sky.

Lost Lagoon is all of these things and more: a place to watch young children run gleefully after birds far wiser than they, a place for lovers to stroll with fingers entwined, a place to jog and cycle or to simply sit and pause for a moment, to reflect, enjoy and possibly even rediscover some part of us we may have forgotten.

A picnic amidst logging debris. Over the years Stanley Park has been coveted by many special interest groups.

THE LAST WORD

Stanley Park is a special place but a fragile one.

This statement may sound strange given the vast tract of peninsula it occupies. Yet this very size may pose the greatest threat to one of the world's most magnificent urban parks. It was dedicated to the enjoyment of all people over a century ago but few then could have appreciated just how literally succeeding generations would take that promise.

During the intervening years, special-interest groups have lobbied unceasingly for their own piece or vision of Stanley Park, not with a view to destroying it but in the mistaken belief that its ability to meet all needs was infinite. It wasn't and isn't.

Stanley Park was a virtual wilderness in 1888, but anyone who saw it then would be staggered by the changes in a handful of generations.

Much of the forest has been whittled away, victim of sports fields, zoos, an aquarium, golf course, tennis courts, roadways, parking lots and more. Taken piecemeal, these developments seemed minor and manageable. In the aggregate, their impact has been enormous. And still the pressure continues.

Sight-seeing tallyho in the early 1900s. The tradition continues,
with today's horse-drawn tallyho very popular.

The vehicle below beside the Hollow Tree in 1911 is believed to be
the first motor-driven, sight-seeing vehicle in Vancouver.

Residents of Vancouver and the surrounding Lower Mainland account for most of the millions of visitors and many more millions of vehicles which enter the park annually. Their numbers are increasing, yet Stanley Park never can be any larger than it is now.

This problem is not restricted to Stanley Park but afflicts all Lower Mainland park systems. If, for example, we have 1,000 acres or hectares of park and a population of 1,000, the ratio of park space to people is 1:1. If park space remains constant but the population doubles, the ratio is halved.

This decline is precisely what is happening in the Vancouver parks and recreation system and its neighbors. The amount of dedicated park space has changed comparatively little, yet the number of area residents and tourists has soared.

As a consequence, parks and recreation opportunities are steadily decreasing. Future generations will never know the degree of park space we have now, and the space for each succeeding generation will be less than the one which preceded it.

This factor is already evident in Stanley Park.

Its very popularity, both as passive green space and a recreation area, has resulted in such a great influx of people that their latitude to indulge in either facet has diminished — and will diminish further. This glorious Park cannot, to paraphrase a politician's grandiloquent boast, be all things to all people for all time. Limits of some kind are essential to ensure that it survives in something resembling its present form for those generations to come.

Unlike a park which exists solely as a recreational area and is, appropriately, tailored to meet the specific needs of users, Stanley Park should be quite the opposite. The needs of the Park should dictate what uses can be made of it.

This view now seems to have been more or less accepted (if not actually stated) by Parks Officials and groups planning the future of Stanley Park. The former, however, may be handicapped to some extent by the fact that they are elected and subject to political pressure. Actions they endorse for the preservation of the Park will undoubtedly be unpopular in some quarters, even though prohibitions or restrictions of some sort now seem inevitable.

The key to guaranteeing the viability of Stanley Park lies in weighing the demands of special-interest groups, whose vociferous posturing may be disproportionate to their representation in the general community, against the need to sustain the Park in the long term.

It will require firmness on the part of Parks Board members, the support of the public, and responsible soul-searching by any person or organization seeking recognition for claims on Stanley Park's limited resources.

Considering what is at stake, a few sacrifices are a minor price for any of us to pay. Our children, our grandchildren, and all other future generations will thank us for our foresight.

ACKNOWLEDGEMENTS

This book is a hybrid. The root stock was the author's guide "The Stanley Park Explorer" published in 1985.

Credit for this new book goes to Art Downs at Heritage House Publishing. So thanks are deservedly due to Art and his small but dedicated staff who are among the most consistently cheerful and helpful individuals I've encountered in the B.C. publishing world.

Tipping the hat to everyone else is a problem since so many assisted with both the earlier book and this one. In all, over 100 individuals contributed. Still, it's worth the attempt.

Carol deFina, Terri Clarke and Pieter Rutgers at the Vancouver Board of Parks and Recreation were efficient and responsive to what were sometimes urgent requests for statistics and background details critical to this book's accuracy.

Thanks must also go to the staffs at the Museum of Anthropology at UBC, B.C. Provincial Museum, Provincial Archives, City of Vancouver Archives, Vancouver Public Library, Heritage Conservation Branch, Special Collections (UBC), Vancouver Museum, and the Powell River Historical Museum.

Special assistance was also rendered by the Vancouver Public Aquarium's Marisa Nichini, and by members of the Vancouver Historical Society and the Vancouver Natural History Society.

I'm also thankful for the opportunity to correct a regrettable and boorish oversight in this book's predecessor by recognizing the decisions of editors at *The Vancouver Sun* and *The Province* newspapers to run my pleas for assistance from the general public. The response was overwhelming and were the chief source of the personal anecdotes recounted in both editions.

The enthusiastic support this project received from Gerry O'Neil of AAA Horse & Carriage went far beyond the call of duty, good entrepreneurship or even friendship. I shudder to think how many hours and dollars you contributed to this book, Gerry, to ensure that I got the cover photograph I wanted.

Others who gave unstintingly of their valuable time included former Stanley Park Zoo Curator, Larry LeSage; the current Curator, Mike MacIntosh; Don Van Dyke, Vic Kondrosky, George Wainborn and former Superintendent of Parks, Stu Lefeaux; Don Abbott, Brian Young, Walter Bishop, Jack Carver, Don Burton, Tom Grant, Danny Veitch, Art Charlton, Robert Cole and family, Frances Woodward, Leif Gunderson, Wilfred Gonsalves and family, Herman Leisk, Doris Lundy, Laurel "Buddy" McDermott, David Rosen, Scotty Neish, Joe Swan, Arthur Reid, Christopher Richardson, Joyce Loft, Randy Stoltman, J. M. Thornton and Mary McDowell.

Sadly, some are no longer with us — but I thank you all.

BIBLIOGRAPHY

Many different sources were consulted in the process of researching this project: the photographic "morgue" at Pacific Press, Parks Board minutes at the City of Vancouver Archives, and newspaper files at the Vancouver Public Library among others. A partial list of book sources includes:

Berton, Pierre *The Last Spike*, Toronto; McClelland & Stewart, 1971.

Berton, Pierre *The National Dream*, Toronto; McClelland & Stewart, 1973.

Carver, J. A. *The Vancouver Rowing Club*, Vancouver; Aubrey F. Roberts Ltd., 1980.

Cruise, David & Griffiths, Alison *The Lords of the Line*, New York; Viking, 1988.

Marsh, James H., Ed. *The Canadian Encyclopedia*, 2nd Ed., Vol. I, 2; Edmonton; Hurtig Publishers, 1988.

Davis, Chuck *The Vancouver Book*,Vancouver; J.J. Douglas, 1976.

Godfrey, W. Earl *The Birds of Canada*, Ottawa; National Museum of Canada, 1970.

Gun, S.W.A. *A Complete Guide To The Totem Poles of Stanley Park*, Vancouver; W.E.G. MacDonald, 1965.

Hood, R.A. *By Shore and Trail in Stanley Park*, Toronto; McClelland & Stewart, 1929.

Matthews, Maj. J.S. *Conversations With Khatsahlano*, Vancouver; City of Vancouver Archives, 1955.

Matthews, Maj. J.S. *Early Vancouver*, Vancouver; City of Vancouver Archives, 1953.

Maud, Ralph *The Salish People, The Local Contribution of Charles Hill-Tout*, Vancouver; Talon Books, 1978.

McKelvie, B.A. *Legends of Stanley Park*, 1941.

Moogk, Peter N. *Vancouver Defended, A History of the Men and Guns of the Lower Mainland Defences, 1859-1949*, Vancouver; Antonson Publishing, 1978.

Morley, Alan *Vancouver: Milltown to Metropolis*, Vancouver; Mitchell Press, 3rd ed., 1974.

Nicol, Eric *Vancouver*, Toronto; Doubleday, 1970.

Pickford, A.E. *Archaeological Excavation of Indian Middens*, Victoria, 1947.

Steele, Richard Michael *The First 100 Years*, Vancouver; the Vancouver Board of Parks and Recreation, 1988.

Thornton, J.M. *H.M.C.S. Discovery and Deadman's Island*, Vancouver, 1975.

Woodcock, George *British Columbia - A History of the Province*, Vancouver; Douglas & McIntyre, 1990.

INDEX

Siwash Rock is a prominent landmark on the Seawall, a spectacular 8.9-km (5.5-mile) footpath unique in Canada.

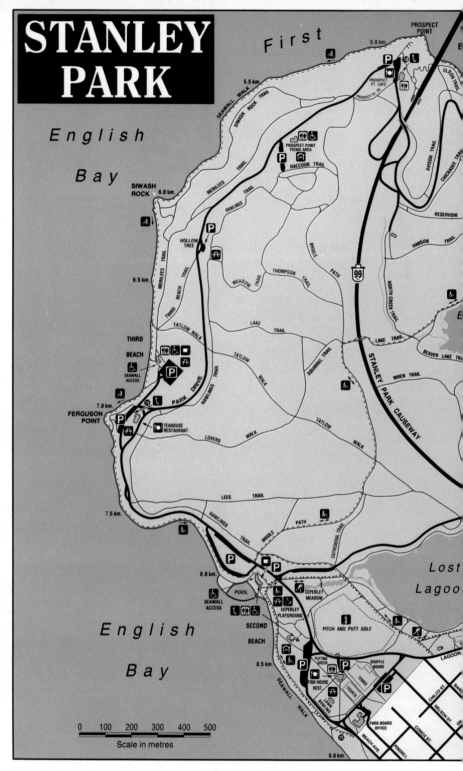

STANLEY PARK

English

Bay

First

PROSPECT POINT

5.0 km.

SEAWALL WALK

SIWASH ROCK TRAIL

5.5 km.

PROSPECT PT. 1R

PROSPECT PT. CAFE

MERILEES TRAIL

PROSPECT POINT PICNIC AREA

RACCOON TRAIL

SIWASH ROCK 6.0 km.

RAWLINGS TRAIL

ELDON TRAIL

AVISON TRAIL

CHICKADEE TRAIL

RESERVOIR

HOLLOW TREE

MEADOW TRAIL

THOMPSON TRAIL

BRIDLE PATH

HANSON TRAIL

99

MERILEES TRAIL

6.5 km.

THIRD BEACH TRAIL

TATLOW WALK

LAKE TRAIL

NORTH CREEK TRAIL

THIRD

BEACH

SEAWALL ACCESS

TATLOW WALK

SQUIRREL TRAIL

LAKE TRAIL

BEAVER LAKE TRAIL

WREN TRAIL

RAWLINGS TRAIL

STANLEY PARK CAUSEWAY

7.0 km.

FERGUSON POINT

PARK DRIVE

TEAHOUSE RESTAURANT

LOVERS WALK

TATLOW WALK

LEES TRAIL

Lost

Lagoo

7.5 km.

RAWLINGS TRAIL

BRIDLE PATH

CATHEDRAL TRAIL

8.0 km.

SEAWALL ACCESS

POOL

CEPERLEY MEADOW

CEPERLEY PLAYGROUND

PITCH AND PUTT GOLF

LAGOON

English

SECOND BEACH

8.5 km.

PUTTING GREEN

SHUFFLE BOARD

TENNIS

CHILCO ST.

NELSON ST.

Bay

SEAWALL WALK

FISH HOUSE REST.

LAWN BOWLING

COURT

PARK BOARD OFFICE

COMOX ST.

BEACH AVE.

PENDRELL

| 0 | 100 | 200 | 300 | 400 | 500 |

Scale in metres

9.0 km.

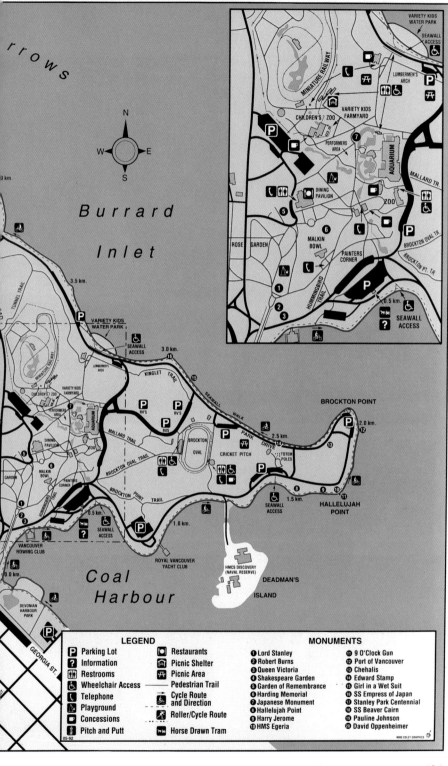

LEGEND

P Parking Lot	**◎** Restaurants
? Information	**🏠** Picnic Shelter
👫 Restrooms	**🏕** Picnic Area
♿ Wheelchair Access	—— Pedestrian Trail
☎ Telephone	– – Cycle Route and Direction
🧒 Playground	···· Roller/Cycle Route
🍴 Concessions	**🐴** Horse Drawn Tram
⛳ Pitch and Putt	

MONUMENTS

❶ Lord Stanley	⓫ 9 O'Clock Gun
❷ Robert Burns	⓬ Port of Vancouver
❸ Queen Victoria	⓭ Chehalis
❹ Shakespeare Garden	⓮ Edward Stamp
❺ Garden of Remembrance	⓯ Girl in a Wet Suit
❻ Harding Memorial	⓰ SS Empress of Japan
❼ Japanese Monument	⓱ Stanley Park Centennial
❽ Hallelujah Point	⓲ SS Beaver Cairn
❾ Harry Jerome	⓳ Pauline Johnson
❿ HMS Egeria	⓴ David Oppenheimer

05-92

MIKE EDLEY GRAPHICS

Opposite page: Among nearly 50 points of interest on the Seawall are Girl in Wetsuit, Lord Stanley's statue and the Lava Cliffs below Prospect Point which are home to a large seabird colony, with pelagic cormorants predominant.

The other photo on the opposite page is a Humboldt penguin called Brunswick. Raised from a chick, it is the Park's goodwill ambassador.

The iguana, opposite, is one of over 8,000 live specimens in the Vancouver Public Aquarium in Stanley Park. An interactive classroom for children of all ages, the Aquarium is probably the Park's most popular attraction.

The Variety Kids Waterpark, below, is free and open all summer.

The totem poles are a major Stanley Park attraction. All are
authentic, with new poles carved on the site.

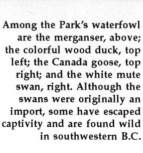

Among the Park's waterfowl
are the merganser, above;
the colorful wood duck, top
left; the Canada goose, top
right; and the white mute
swan, right. Although the
swans were originally an
import, some have escaped
captivity and are found wild
in southwestern B.C.

The flamingo, opposite, is an import from the tropics but the great blue heron and the mallard duck, below, are familiar B.C. residents.

A Rocky Mountain bighorn sheep and an Orca, better known as the killer whale, are among B.C.'s mammals in the Park. The Orca's nickname of "killer" is unjustified since there is no record of it ever harming a human being.

The South American cayman, above, and the Arctic Ocean beluga whale, below, show the diversity of the Aquarium's wildlife species.

The sea otter, opposite, was once abundant on the B.C. Coast but was hunted to extinction for its fur. It now has been re-established.

Sunset on Second Beach, a smelt fisherman in the foreground. The inset photo is of Third Beach, in the background one of the many majestic cruise ships which visit Vancouver every summer.

Winter doesn't
diminish the
popularity of
Stanley Park, its
ducks, swans,
raccoons, squirrels
and other wildlife
are still there to
welcome visitors.

In an average winter, snow remains in the Park for only a few days, creating a Christmas postcard of scenery.
At top left, opposite page, is the Seawall near Second Beach; above, the shore of Lost Lagoon; and, opposite, a panorama of English Bay from the Second Beach entrance.

Seasonal floral beds like the one
above add splashes of color to the
Park. The top display is in front of
the rose garden cottage.

The wild skunk cabbage, despite
its unflattering name, is a cheerful
herald of spring, its bright yellow
flower a miniature sun amidst the
dark debris of winter.